REA's
Quick & Easy Guide to

Writing & Publishing Your

Scientific / Technical Paper

Staff of Research & Education Association
Dr. M. Fogiel, Director

Research & Education Association

61 Ethel Road West, Piscataway, New Jersey 08854

REA's Quick & Easy Guide to
WRITING AND PUBLISHING YOUR
A+ SCIENTIFIC / TECHNICAL PAPER

Printed in the United States of America

Library of Congress Catalog Card Number 96-72492

International Standard Book Number 0-87891-913-9

RESEARCH & EDUCATION ASSOCIATION
61 Ethel Road West
Piscataway, New Jersey 08854

CONTENTS

Chapter 3
GOOD FORM AND USAGE

Chapter 4
TABLES

Chapter 5
ILLUSTRATIONS

Chapter 6
PREPUBLICATION REVIEW / STEPS

Chapter 7
PROOFREADING

Preface

This manual is intended to meet the practical needs of students and research workers who are preparing papers on scientific or technical subjects. The student who is confronted with the arduous task of "writing up" his data will find in this book many suggestions that should not only lighten his work, but enable him to present his material in a more effective way.

Writing is an essential part of the scientist's profession. The final and in some respects the most important stage in any scientific investigation is the preparation of the results for publication. After a scientific or technical worker has done a good piece of research work, he should present it to his colleagues in the best possible form. Failure to do so, as may be noted in many cases, may largely discount the value of the work itself. The average technical specialist tends to think that his work is done when the research project as such is finished, and to regard the publication as an unnecessary evil and a nuisance. As Charles Darwin expressed it, "A naturalist's life would be a happy one if he had only to observe and never to write."

Few people, in fact, like to write. Certainly few are able to write easily, and those who can sit down and dash off a good scientific paper in a few hours are indeed rare. The time factor is far more important than the beginner in science is likely to realize. Most candidates for the doctorate should devote at least three months to the writing of a dissertation running to the usual length of about 40 typewritten pages. The scientist is judged solely by the quality of his final product. No one will criticize him for spending many hours on his manuscript and carrying it through several revisions to make it as nearly perfect as possible.

Unless research workers are willing to learn to write effectively, each scientific or technical institution may need to have on its staff someone whose duty it is to edit and, if necessary, ghostwrite publications on work done in the institution. Few scientists, however, would welcome such a procedure.

It may be true that the average technical specialist is unwilling or unable to write properly. But this does not apply to leaders in science. If the student will survey the history of science, he cannot fail to note a high degree of correlation between ability in writing and achievement in science.

Proficiency in writing—like skill in laboratory manipulation—can be gained through study and practice. This should not be too difficult for the science student, once he realizes that with practice, and constant effort toward improvement, he can achieve success.

Every student who is preparing for work in science should realize as early as possible that such training is a highly important part of his education. In recording the results of laboratory experiments, the student has abundant opportunity for acquiring this skill. Thus,

> "The chief purpose of a laboratory training is not to teach the students how to use elaborate instruments or to perform complicated chemical tests. The incalculable gift of the laboratory is its discipline in scientific method, and its training in the importance of logical reasoning and the use of exact language in speaking and in writing. The scientist is always distinguished from the empiricist by his accuracy in measurement, by his precision in statement, by his honesty in accepting and handling evidence, and by his fairness in presenting it when contesting the opinions of those in opposition to his own views."

The student should learn to write as accurately, clearly, and concisely as possible. To make rapid improvement, he should apply the knowledge he has gained in the study of English composition and should frequently consult a handbook that deals specifically with scientific writing. The benefit derived from this work will be increased if each report is carefully revised before it is submitted in its final form. No single factor is more important than daily practice. Translating from a foreign language and reading good books, slowly, are also helpful.

Several meetings of the departmental seminar for graduate students might profitably be devoted to a discussion of the preparation of scientific results for publication. Each member of the group could report on a phase of the subject in which he is especially interested or competent. To emphasize the points discussed, the reports should be illustrated with examples of good and of poor work selected from the current literature of the science. Techniques used in preparing graphs, drawings, and photographs could be demonstrated by members of the group or by other persons who have acquired skill in these arts. Visits to a printing plant which may be arranged for a small party in nearly any city, would give the group first-hand information on the final steps in the production of printed matter.

This guide to the preparation and writing of scientific papers should be a convenient aid to students and others engaged in scientific work. It has served as a style manual for theses, dissertations, journal articles, and monographs; and it has been used as a supplementary textbook in English courses. This book is the result of a process of development and adaptation.

The material in this book is a revised and updated version of "The Scientific Paper" by Sam F. Trelease.

CHAPTER 1

The Research Problem

Choosing A Research Problem[1]

In choosing a research problem, special knowledge of a particular field of science is indispensable. The selection of a problem requires study, thought, and planning—guided by all the imagination, originality, and critical judgment at the command of the investigator.

Many scientists find it helpful to accumulate a list, in the form of a card index, of promising research problems from which selection may be made. It is advantageous to make a tentative analysis of each subject, indicating briefly the object, scope, general plan of investigation, and probable nature of the results that might be obtained.

The criteria given below should be useful in stimulating search and thought during the preliminary survey of possible research problems in an experimental phase of science. Although the criteria are purposely stated in the form of brief rules, it will be understood that they are to be regarded merely as hints or suggestions, which, though helpful in many cases, are obviously not universally applicable.

1. The problem should deal, usually in a quantitative way, with the relations between natural phenomena—or, more specifically, with the causal conditions that control observable facts or events.

2. It should be circumscribed, definite, and specific, but should preferably lead far into the literature.

---

1. Dr. Burton E. Livingston helped in the preparation of this section.

1

3. It should be capable of statement in the form of several alternative hypotheses, each of which may be tested in order.

4. It should be capable of experimental treatment with the knowledge and facilities available, and it should give promise of yielding definite and reliable results within the allotted time.

5. It should have as its primary object the obtaining of new facts and conclusions in a specific field, preferably on a topic possessing importance to the science as a whole.

6. It should give promise of leading to other interesting and important problems, and should prepare the investigator for handling them.

7. It should usually test some proposition about which there is difference of opinion, or one that has secured acceptance upon logically insufficient grounds.

8. It may well deal with the salient features of some little-known relation, rather than with the details of some better-known and more thoroughly analyzed subject.

9. It may take up some question that has been relatively neglected.

10. It should deal with materials well adapted to the proposed experimentation, preference perhaps being given to those widely known or economically important.

Using The Library[2]

For a research worker, the library plays a very important role. The planning, interpreting, and reporting of original research are all dependent on knowledge of the literature published by others in the same field. This section endeavors to give an introduction to the use of the library and to draw attention to some of the important works to be found there.

1. The Catalogue. The catalogue is the key to the library collections. Large libraries often have separate catalogues for certain collections. This is confusing to the user. For example, medicine and law may not appear in the general catalogue; collections of doctoral dissertations

---

2. Prepared by Miss Amy L. Hepburn, of the Columbia University Library.

may be found in special libraries with a separate card index; and manuscripts may be in a file by themselves. It is best to inquire at the reference desk if you fail to find what you wish.

When consulting the catalogue, it would be advantageous to find out what special filing rules may have been followed. For example, one would expect to find the items alphabetized *word by word*. Thus, *New York* should come before *Newfoundland*. But some catalogues have the cards filed *letter by letter;* in these, *Newark* would appear before *New York*. Libraries also differ in the case of *Mc* and *Mac*. It seems simpler to have all under *Mac*, but this method is not always followed. Usually libraries do not file under prepositions in surnames, as *von* and *de*; but a preposition and an article, as *du*, is recognized as preceding the rest of the surname. To make doubly sure when in doubt, try both ways. Hyphenated names generally come under the first part of the surname, as *Page-Wood, John*. When an author changes her name by marriage, the name under which the author first wrote is most commonly used; but there should be a cross reference under the married name. Libraries differ in regard to the German umlaut; *Müller* may be filed under *Muller* or *Mueller*.

In locating serials—a term which includes periodicals, journals, magazines, or publications of societies, institutions, etc.—the best rules to follow are those which appear in the first part of the *Union List of Serials in Libraries of the United States and Canada*. To quote:

> A serial not published by a society or a public office is entered under the first word, not an article, of the latest form of the title.

> A serial published by a society, but having a distinctive title, is entered under the title, with reference from the name of the society.

> The journals, transactions, proceedings, etc., of a society are entered under the first word, not an article, of the latest form of the name of the society.

> Learned societies and academies of Europe, other than English, with names beginning with an adjective denoting

royal privilege are entered under the first word following the adjective (Kaiserlich, Königlich, Reale, Imperiale, etc.).

If you have an abbreviated title that is difficult to understand, consult the *World List of Scientific Periodicals*, published by the Oxford University Press, and also the volume listing abbreviations. This list is arranged alphabetically by the first word of the title, not an article. It is especially useful when a puzzling foreign reference is involved. Special subjects have their own lists of explanations of abbreviations, as those in *Chemical Abstracts, Biological Abstracts,* and *Science Abstracts.*

Government documents present a complexity all their own in the catalogue. The United States probably issues more publications than any other nation. The comprehensive cumulative indexes published by the government should be used in locating a difficult reference. Monthly lists with a yearly index bring the file up to date. In spite of this aid an appeal often has to be made to the reference department for assistance in locating a document in the catalogue; so too much time should not be expended before soliciting help.

2. Classifications. Libraries are classified in order to bring together publications on a particular subject. The two most familiar classifications are the *Dewey decimal system* and the *Library of Congress system.*

The *Dewey decimal system* is a numerical arrangement whereby a number can be expanded by means of a decimal. For example, *General Science* is designated by the number 500, *Chemistry* by 540, *Organic Chemistry* by 547, while further divisions would make use of the decimal as 547.1, 547.2, etc. There are infinite possibilities for expansion. Under this *class number*, as it is called, a symbol is added, called the *Cutter number,* which stands for the author. If the author is *Smith*, you will find *Sm 5* or *Sm 55*. These numbers are decimals. *Sm 55* would stand just before *Sm 551.* Thus a book on organic chemistry might have a number like this:

547.11
Sm 55

The *Library of Congress system* classifies by the use of letters. The first letter indicates the class; the second a division of the class; and further sectioning is made by the use of numbers. For example, the letter *Q* stands for *Science, QC* for *Physics,* and *QC* 252-333 for *Heat.*

Although both schemes may look complicated, they afford the library a means of bringing together on the shelf the publications on a certain subject. This is particularly valuable to the research worker who has an opportunity to visit the shelves to consult familiar books and become acquainted with those that are new to him.

It is most important that the *call number,* the number appearing in the upper left-hand corner of the catalogue card, be copied in full when requesting a book. An *F* under the Cutter number, as:

> 547.2
> D15
> F

would mean folio size, and this very large book would undoubtedly be shelved in another place from books of medium size. Sometimes, a volume number is added, as:

> 590.6
> Un 33
> vol. 7

This means that the reference you have found is in a certain volume of a series, and the volume number must be included when requesting the book.

3. Subject Headings. The subject approach to the catalogue should be more generally emphasized. The subjects that appear at the top of the card are selected by specialists in certain fields. But as time goes on, the headings may not be revised; so new developments may be filed under antiquated headings. Under the subject heading, the person using the catalogue will find grouped together the works on the particular subject in which he is interested. Thus publications on the intricate life processes of plants are under *Botany—Physiological.* Again, the reference department should come to your aid if you are doubtful under which subject heading you should look. Most libraries depend upon the headings selected by the Library of Congress, but some choose their own.

In this brief introduction to the catalogue, an attempt has been made to show that catalogues vary. Failing to find your reference in one place, try other possibilities and then ask someone in the reference department. Difficult foreign names or obscure abbreviations for periodicals may present problems in which only the reference department can help you.

First Steps In Treating Data

1. Tables. Check all calculations, and put experimental data in the form of tables. (See chapter on "Tables," page 76.) Make all calculations twice, preferably on different days, and, if practicable, by different methods. The second calculation should be made without reference to the first, and on a new page in your notebook. Notes on observational and descriptive work should be arranged and classified.

2. Graphs. Plot your data wherever possible. In most experimentation, graphs furnish the best means of bringing out relations among data, and should be prepared even if they are not to be published.

It is advisable to keep the data tabulated and plotted as the experimentation progresses. This will serve to check the accuracy of the work; it will indicate desirable modifications in the plan; and it is likely to suggest valuable new ideas.

3. Written Notes. During the preliminary study of the data, it is advisable to record on paper all the ideas that seem to be worthy of consideration. The mechanical process of recording and filing the notes should suit the convenience of the individual. Some writers like to use a standard size of cards (5 by 8 inches) for all preliminary work on a paper. The cards may be filed in a box, under appropriate headings. Only one topic is put on a card, and this topic is expanded later to make a paragraph. This method allows topics to be added, eliminated, and rearranged whenever necessary. Other writers prefer to use sheets of paper of standard size ($8^1/_2$ by 11 inches), putting only one topic on a sheet and filing the sheets in folders, large envelopes, or loose-leaf notebooks. (Original observations and measurements are usually recorded in a notebook with permanent pages. A copy should be put in a safe place as soon as possible.)

4. Conclusions. Examine the tables, graphs, and classified notes for relations and conclusions. Ask yourself, "What are the possible explanations of the facts?" If several explanations seem equally probable, do not emphasize *only one*. Consider all logical possibilities. (See section on "Logical Presentation of Ideas," page 21.) Make written notes of tentative conclusions.

If time is available, verify your conclusions by gathering more data or by making special test experiments. Confirm your conclusions, if possible, by evidence from sources that are entirely different in character.

Estimate the probable accuracy of your results by considering the sources of error. Conclusions from your results must be based upon a careful consideration of their accuracy and sufficiency. If you have enough data, use statistical methods to estimate their probable significance.

5. Revision of Conclusions. Refer again to your data to see whether your tentative conclusions are actually justified. Discover in which cases these conclusions apply and in which, if any, they do not. Modify, if necessary, the statement of your conclusions. See also whether they are consistent with established facts or principles pertaining to the subject.

6. Exceptions. Examine the data for exceptions, inconsistencies, and discrepancies. Record the exceptions, and check their values. Try to find out why the expected result was not obtained. Some of the most important scientific discoveries have resulted from apparent exceptions and abnormalities in data.

Formulate possible explanations for the exceptions.

Study your conclusions again to see how the exceptions modify them.

Reliability and Significance of Measurements

This section provides a brief introduction to some aspects of statistical methods. If statistical analysis is to be applied to the results, it is important that the experiments be planned with this in mind. Defects in the design of the experiments may make it difficult or impossible to determine the statistical significance of the results.

The following directions outline a working system for: (a) computing the standard error of the mean of a series of measurements obtained from a sample, (b) ascertaining the significance of the difference between the population mean and the mean of a sample, (c) judging the significance of the difference between two sample means, and (d) estimating the size of an adequate sample.

Standard Error of the Mean

1. Write the readings in a vertical column. At the bottom of the column, write the sum of the readings; divide this by the number of readings (N) and set down the mean (M).

2. In a second column, put opposite each reading the difference between it and the mean.

3. In a third column, write the square of each difference; and at the bottom of this column, put the sum of these squares (S).

4. Compute the standard error of the mean by taking the square root of the quotient obtained by dividing the sum of the squares by the product of the number of readings times one less than this number:

$$E_M = [S/(N(N-1))]^{1/2}$$

5. Write the mean and its standard error in the form $M \pm E_M$. (According to the theory of probabilities, 68 per cent of many similarly determined means, based on large samples, should fall within $\pm E_M$ of the population mean, 95 per cent may be expected to fall within $\pm 1.96\ E_M$, and 99 per cent within $\pm 2.58\ E_M$.)

Significance of the Difference Between a Population Mean and the Mean of a Random Sample

1. Compute n from:

$$n = N-1$$

where N is the number of readings upon which the mean of the random sample was based.

2. Compute the value of t from:

$$t = (M-m)/E_M$$

where M is the mean of the sample, m is the known or assumed value of the population mean, and E_M is the standard error of the mean of the sample.

3. In table 1, find the *smaller* value of t corresponding to n. If the computed value of t is greater than the value of t found in the table, the difference between the population mean and the mean of the sample may be regarded as significant. If the computed value of t exceeds the larger value of t in the table, the difference is highly significant.

TABLE 1

Values of t at P = 0.05 and P = 0.01 for selected values of n (degrees of freedom) from 4 to infinity

	t			t	
n	$P = 0.05$	$P = 0.01$	n	$P = 0.05$	$P = 0.01$
4	2.78	4.60	15	2.13	2.95
5	2.57	4.03	16	2.12	2.92
6	2.45	3.71	17	2.11	2.90
7	2.37	3.50	18	2.10	2.88
8	2.31	3.36	19	2.09	2.86
9	2.26	3.25	20	2.09	2.85
10	2.23	3.17	25	2.06	2.79
11	2.20	3.11	30	2.04	2.75
12	2.18	3.06	40	2.02	2.70
13	2.16	3.01	50	2.01	2.68
14	2.15	2.98	Infinity	1.96	2.58

A significant difference indicates that the sample was probably not drawn from a population having a mean of m, or that the sample was not drawn at random, or both.

Significance of the Difference Between Means

1. Subtract the smaller mean (M_2) from the larger mean (M_1) to obtain the difference (D).

2. Obtain the standard error of the difference between the two means by taking the square root of the sum of the squares of the two standard errors of the means:

$$E_D = [(E_{M_1})^2 + (E_{M_2})^2]^{1/2}$$

where E_{M_1} and E_{M_2} are the standard errors of the means. This expression for E_D should be used only when the two random samples are independent and are about the same size.

3. Write the difference and its standard error in the form $D \pm E_D$.

4. Compute n from:

$$n = (N_1{-}1) + (N_2{-}1)$$

where N_1 and N_2 are the number of readings upon which the means were based.

5. Compute t from $t = D/E_D$. In table 1, find the *smaller* value of t corresponding to n. If the computed ratio is greater than the value of t found in the table, the difference may be considered to be significant. If the ratio exceeds the larger value of t in the table, the difference may be regarded as highly significant. The P (probability) value indicates the probability of obtaining a *plus or minus* difference equal to or greater than that indicated by the value of t.

Adequacy of Sample Size

1. An estimate may be made of the size of each of two samples needed in order that a certain percentage difference between the two sample means may be regarded as significant. For simplicity, it is assumed (a) that the two populations from which the random samples are drawn have the same degree of variability and (b) that the two random samples are independent.

2. Obtain an exploratory random sample of size N (as large as practicable) of one of the two populations, and calculate the mean (M) and the standard error of the mean (E_M).

3. Compute the required sample size (N_r) for each of the two samples from the following formula:

$$N_r = 2 \times (2.16)^2 \times N \times (100 \times E_M/M)^2/d^2$$

10

where 2.16 is a value obtained from a t table and corresponds to a probability of 0.03 for a large sample, and d is the percentage difference desired to be significant.

4. It must be borne in mind that the procedure here outlined can give only a rough estimate of adequate sample size and should not be used for small samples.

CHAPTER 2

Writing the Paper

Outline of a Scientific Paper

1. Scientific Writing. A paper on a scientific or technical subject necessarily consists of (a) a report of facts, (b) an interpretation of facts, or (c) a combination of a report and an interpretation. The method of writing is governed by many conditions, including the nature of the subject, the purpose of the article, the characteristics of the writer, and the interests of the probable readers. No set method or arrangement will be suited to all kinds of papers.

It is important that the plan of the composition be made very clear to the reader. The main topics and their subdivisions should be plainly indicated. In this respect scientific writing differs from literary composition. A scientific paper is intended to be studied and used as a reference; it is not merely to be read. Hence, literary devices should be subordinated if they interfere with clearness. The plan should be self-evident throughout the composition.

2. General Outline. The outline given below suggests a form that may be used for a wide variety of scientific and technical papers. An examination of the papers published in the journals will show that the majority of them have this general arrangement and sequence of topics. This form of outline is suitable for most papers that report investigations or experiments, and possesses the additional advantage of being familiar to the reader. The outline should be modified sufficiently to adapt it to the special requirements of the article or report that is to be written.

General Outline of a Scientific Paper

TITLE. The title should consist preferably of few words, indicative of the contents that are most emphasized. Great care must be exercised to employ words that contain the elements both of brevity and comprehensiveness to permit easy and accurate indexing.

ABSTRACT. The abstract is a brief condensation of the whole paper.

I. *Introduction.*

    A. Nature of the problem; its state at the beginning of the investigation.

    B. Purpose, scope, and method of the investigation.

    C. Most significant outcome of the investigation; the state of the problem at the end of the investigation.

II. *Materials and methods.*

    A. Description of the equipment and materials employed.

    B. Explanation of the way in which the work was done. (Give sufficient detail to enable a competent worker to repeat your experiments. Emphasize the features that are new.)

III. *Experiments and results.*

    A. Description of the experiments.

    B. Description of the results. (If possible, these should be shown in tables and graphs.)

IV. *Discussion of results.*

    A. Main principles, causal relations, or generalizations that are shown by the results. (Choose one or several main conclusions which your evidence tends to prove.)

    B. Evidence (as shown by the data) for each of the main conclusions.

    C. Exceptions and opposing theories, and explanations of these.

D. Comparison of your results and interpretations with those of other workers.

Outline of a paper, that includes several series of experiments, is advantageous to present separately.

TITLE.

ABSTRACT.

I. *General introduction.*

II. *General materials and methods.*

III. *Descriptive title of first series of experiments.*

    A. Introduction.

    B. Materials and methods.

    C. Experiments and results.

    D. Discussion of results.

IV. *Descriptive title of second series of experiments.*

    A. Introduction.

    B. Materials and methods.

    C. Experiments and results.

    D. Discussion of results.

V. *Descriptive title of third series of experiments.*

    A. Introduction.

    B. Materials and methods.

    C. Experiments and results.

    D. Discussion of results.

VI. *General discussion.*

Process of Writing

1. Mechanical Process. There probably is no best way to prepare a scientific paper, except as may be determined by the individual writer and the circumstances. With no notes at all, one might be able to start writing an article which, short or long, would be practically finished at every stage; or one might accumulate the facts in a great mass of verbiage, and then, through condensation and revision, put the paper into final form. It is the end product that counts, not the intermediate steps.

2. Preliminary Outline. Most people obtain best results by developing a preliminary outline before they start writing. The following steps may be employed:

(a)   Prepare a brief outline of the topics to be treated in your article. Arrange the topics in a convenient and logical order. This outline may be on a single sheet of paper.

(b)   Make a second, enlarged outline showing an analysis, by headings and subheadings, of the article. This may be three or four times as long as the first.

(c)   Prepare a third outline before beginning the actual writing. In this outline the topics should be shifted to the most effective order, and each topic should be enlarged and preferably expressed in the form of a concise topic sentence.

(d)   Begin the actual writing. Spread out before you the outline, the tables, and the graphs. Expand each topic or topic sentence of the outline into a paragraph. Make a rough draft first. Concentrate on the subject matter, and write as rapidly as possible, without letting details of language interrupt the flow of ideas. Then, on another day, examine critically what you have written and begin to revise it. (See section on "Revising the Manuscript," page 24.)

Subject Matter and Arrangement

General

1. Unity. A scientific paper should be a unit, treating a single definite subject; it may contain several main topics if these are logical divisions of one large subject. Make a careful selection of materials. Include only what is necessary to an understanding of the main ideas, but omit nothing that is essential.

Each paragraph should have unity. It may well begin with a topic sentence that indicates the idea to be developed in the paragraph. The use of topic sentences aids the writer in transforming his preliminary outline into paragraphs, and it helps the reader who looks through the paper for its salient contents.

2. Arrangement of Topics. Choose a logical sequence of topics, based upon a careful analysis of the subject matter. The order may be determined by relations of space, time, importance, similarity or contrast, complexity, or cause and effect. Use an order that serves best the needs of clearness, coherence, and emphasis. Discuss similar points in the same order, and use similar forms of expression. Indicate clearly the beginning of each new topic.

3. Development. Develop the main ideas until they are clear enough to be easily understood by the reader. For the sake of brevity in publication, it is usually necessary to address the paper to specialists in the particular field, rather than to the general reader. Use the style of the textbook—not that of the laboratory notebook. Present the material in a manner that will enable the reader to grasp it as quickly and easily as possible. Explain each topic clearly, point by point. Define, explain, illustrate, prove, and summarize your statements, if necessary. Give considerable thought to the relative importance of the various topics and their need of development. Treat briefly those topics that are too simple to require detailed explanation. Develop fully the more complex and the more important topics. Achieve completeness and clarity without sacrificing conciseness.

4. Examples. Illustrate the meaning of general or abstract statements by giving examples, particular instances, concrete data, amplifying details, or specific comparisons.

5. Reader's Questions. Consider what questions the reader will wish answered in your article. Always keep in mind the fact that the primary purpose of your paper should be to give the reader valuable information and new ideas.

6. Topics of General Interest. Develop fully the topics that are of interest to many readers.

7. Words. Employ words that are approved by good usage. Be careful to avoid those that are obscure, ambiguous, or inappropriate. Consult *Soule's Dictionary of English Synonyms* or *Webster's Dictionary of Synonyms* when at a loss for the word or expression that most precisely fits your thought, and turn to *The Concise Oxford Dictionary* when in doubt regarding the idiomatic use of common words. With a large vocabulary at your command, one word may take the place of several in making your meaning clear. Try to use words that a foreigner will be able to find in a small dictionary. (For example, a foreigner might not be able to find the meaning of the word "tumbler," but he would understand if you described it as a "cylindrical glass vessel, 7 cm. in diameter and 10 cm. deep.")

Define all technical terms that the reader might not understand.

8. Tone. Skill may be developed in presenting material in a tactful way. Clear statements supported by evidence are better than positive assertions. Avoid pedantic or pompous language. Be careful also not to announce a well-known fact as if it were a discovery. Indicate clearly which of your results and conclusions are new. For completeness of discussion, it is often necessary to mention to the reader many things that he already knows; but this may be done skillfully, without annoying or confusing him.

Title

1. Choice of Title. Choose a concise descriptive title, complete enough to include the main topics needed for making a subject index in an abstract journal. Select these topics with the aim of giving definite ideas as to the exact contents of your paper. In a biological study, it is desirable to give the name of the organism in the title. If necessary, sacrifice brevity in order to include all important nouns under which your paper should be indexed. Place the more important words near the beginning of the title.

2. Selection of Topics. Ask yourself, "Under what topics would I look in a subject index of an abstract journal if I were searching for the literature on the subjects treated in my paper?" The answer to this question will provide the topics for your title.

Introduction

1. Content. The function of the introduction is to make clear the subject of the article. The introduction should state the problem, describe its condition at the beginning of the study, and tell the reasons for investigating it. It should give the purpose, scope, and general method of the investigation.

Finally, the introduction should state clearly and definitely the most significant result of the investigation. With the main conclusion before him at the start, the reader is able, as he goes through the paper, to judge the development of evidence and inference brought forward in its support. If, on the other hand, the statement of the main point is deferred until late in the paper, the reader is unable to distinguish essential from non-essential evidence and may overlook or forget important features.

2. Pertinent Literature. Make reference in the introduction to only those literature citations that bear directly upon the introduction itself. The other references to the literature should be included in the parts of the paper to which they are most pertinent, chiefly the discussion of results.

The foregoing procedure is now favored by most writers. To be sure, a long historical review—often arranged merely chronologically—was at one time considered to be an essential part of the introduction. But the reader generally finds such a review dull, since he is not prepared so early in the paper to correlate past investigations with the specific problem in hand. The place for most of the references to the literature is in the discussion of results, where the new results and interpretations are compared with those of previous investigators.

Discussion of Results

1. Interpretation. The primary purpose of the discussion of results is to show the relations between the facts that you have observed. Indicate the meaning of the facts, their underlying causes, their effects, and their theoretical implications. Aim, where possible, to explain facts in the symbols or language of mathematics, and according to the laws of physics and chemistry.

2. Reference to Tables and Graphs. In referring to tables and graphs, keep the text free from mere repetition of the detailed data presented in the tables and graphs. Such repetition, except when necessary to show comparisons not obvious in the tables and graphs, confuses the text and makes dull reading. As far as possible, the text should be reserved for comparisons, relations, conclusions, and generalizations.

3. Unsettled Points. Give particular attention to evidence that bears on points concerning which there is difference of opinion among scientists. But avoid personal or controversial language, or expressions likely to excite controversy or retort. Above all, do not impugn the motives of others; motives are irrelevant.

4. Emphasis of Conclusions. Indicate the ways in which the results of your study are related to the science as a whole. Emphasize the additions that it makes, and stress conclusions that modify in a significant way any hypothesis, theory, or principle that has secured general acceptance. Develop with special clearness observations or inferences that seem to be of sufficient importance to deserve mention in a textbook on the subject.

5. Qualification of Conclusions. To prevent misunderstanding, it is necessary to define as clearly as possible the precise conditions to which your conclusions apply. A conclusion should always be stated in such a way as to indicate its range of validity.

Confusion often results from failure to define adequately all influential experimental details. In any experiment or series of experiments the influential conditions may be analyzed conveniently into two groups: (1) those representing the variables specially studied, and (2) those representing the rest of the experimental complex—the influential background or prevailing conditions. The conditions of the first group are assumed to be adequately known and controlled; they are the conditions that are purposely made to differ in certain known ways. For an ideal experiment or experiment series, the conditions of the second group should be as thoroughly known and definitely described as are the primary variables; they should be maintained constant or at least not permitted to vary sufficiently to interfere with the influence of the primary variables.

6. Applications. Indicate the practical applications of your study to agriculture, industry, engineering, medicine, etc.

7. Stimulation. Try to stimulate the reader to further thought and research on the subject of your investigation.

Abstract or Summary

1. Position and Designation. Two practices are followed in the various journals: (a) One is to print an *abstract* (often in distinctive type and without heading) at the beginning of the article, just below the title, where it is most convenient for readers. The modern trend in scientific and technical journals is toward the adoption of this method. (b) The other procedure is to print a *summary* (under this heading) at the end of the article.

This abridgment should be the same in content, whether it is designated as an abstract or as a summary.

2. Purpose. In preparing a title and abstract for an article, it is important to realize that the individual worker glances over many more articles than he has time to read. A title is necessarily short but should be as informative as possible. In cases where the worker is uncertain from the title alone whether the article contains material of interest to him, the abstract is there to help him by telling him more precisely what the article covers. Also, in cases where he is interested only in the main results and conclusions, the abstract gives him this information in brief form and saves him the difficulty of reading the article.

The abstract fills a gap between the title, which may average only about ten words, and the article, which may be ten pages long. It is useful to readers who wish more information than is given by the title and less information than is given by the article. Its purpose, then, is to assist readers (a) by elaborating the title and (b) by condensing the article, thus saving the time of readers who do not require the full contents of the paper. Incidentally, if the abstract is well prepared by the author, it will be suitable for reprinting in an abstract journal.

3. Nature. To serve its purpose, the abstract should indicate clearly all the subjects dealt with in the article, so that no reader interested in only one of these subjects will fail to have his attention directed to it. The abstract should also summarize briefly but clearly the principal new results and conclusions, especially all new information likely to be of interest to readers who are not specialists in the field. The abstract should be well written, so as to be easily read and understood, and should be self-explanatory, complete and clear in itself.

4. Preparation. Keeping in view the dual purpose of the abstract, the writer should read his manuscript carefully, making notes (a) as to the subjects dealt with, particularly subjects concerning which new information is given incidentally, and (b) as to the new results and conclusions reported. Material relating to each subject should then be gathered together; sentences summarizing the material should be written; and finally these sentences should be put together so as to make a well-written abstract—brief, condensed, complete, yet readable.

5. Models. It will be useful to study as models the abstracts given in abstract journals and to try to make abstracts which would be acceptable to such journals.

Logical Presentation of Ideas

Many of the mistakes in scientific papers involve errors in logic. Their avoidance depends chiefly upon a thorough understanding and careful analysis of the ideas that are presented.[3] The following rules apply to some of the most obvious, and yet commonest, mistakes of this type.

1. Requisites of a Good Hypothesis. A hypothesis is a tentative explanation of certain observed facts. It is provisionally adopted to explain these facts and to serve as a guide for further investigation. The requisites of a good hypothesis are the following: (a) It should explain facts that have not hitherto been adequately explained. (b) It should be consistent with all the known facts. (c) It should be no more complex than necessary to account for the phenomena. (d) It should aid the prediction of new facts and relations. (e) It should be susceptible of verification or refutation.

---

3. "However skeptical one may be of the attainment of universal truths, one can never deny that philosophic study means the habit of always seeing an alternative, of not taking the usual for granted, of making conventionalities fluid again, of imagining foreign states of mind. In a word, it means the possession of mental perspective."—*William James.*

2. Illusions. (a) Be careful not to draw conclusions from data involving errors of observation, errors in arithmetic, compensating errors, and systematic and personal errors. (b) Do not use mathematical formulas without clearly understanding their derivation and all the assumptions involved. (c) Be cautious in comparing conclusions based upon experiments in which the influential conditions have been improperly controlled, and therefore not duplicated. (d) Avoid confusing facts with opinions or inferences, not only in the investigation itself but also in preparing results for publication.

3. Too Broad Generalization. (a) Do not draw a conclusion from too few data, nor too broad a conclusion from a limited series of data. (b) Be careful in drawing conclusions that are based on extrapolated curves. (c) Guard against failing to qualify a conclusion, so as to show the limits within which it applies, or the variation which is to be expected. (d) When you indulge in speculation, be sure that you, and your reader, know that it is speculation.

4. Cause and Effect. (a) Do not infer merely because one thing has followed another that it is the effect of the other. (b) Do not argue that causes are the same because indistinguishable effects have been observed. A certain phenomenon may have one cause in one case and another cause in a second case. (c) Be careful in making inferences by analogy. If two cases are observed to resemble each other in certain particulars, it is not safe to infer resemblance in another particular that has been noted in only one of them. (d) If two processes have the same mathematical expression (or yield the same sort of graph when plotted), it does not necessarily follow that the processes themselves are essentially alike.

5. Prejudice. (a) An attitude of intellectual honesty and devotion to truth is the foundation of scientific work. (b) Guard against prejudice; do not be influenced by preconceived opinions. (c) Do not decline to admit evidence because it necessitates an unwelcome conclusion. If a conclusion is unwelcome, it is a sign of a wrong mental attitude. (d) Biting, caustic comments are almost sure to be regretted later, and they invariably weaken the effect of one's arguments.

6. Ambiguity of Terms. (a) Guard against misunderstandings of language. (b) Define terms as clearly and precisely as possible. Do not use technical terms, especially in a field not strictly your own, unless you are certain of their precise meaning, or unless their use has been checked by a specialist in the field. (c) Do not use a term in one sense in one part of your reasoning and in another sense in another part. (d) Do not mistake a general for a specific use of a term. (e) Be very critical of statements containing the words *cause, determine, control, influence, result, effect.* Distinguish carefully between such words as *factor, condition, force, agency, process.*

7. Missing the Point. (a) Do not ignore the question, evade the issue, or argue beside the point. Define clearly the points at issue. Try to determine the crucial point that will really decide the discussion. (b) Guard against reasoning that may correctly prove something but not the thing which you think it proves.

8. Begging the Question. (a) Do not base a conclusion on an unproved proposition. (b) Avoid arguing in a circle—drawing a conclusion that merely states the assumptions in other words. (c) Do not assume the truth of a proposition that is not proved and may be false. (d) Do not assume that a certain thing is true because a prominent authority has said it is true. (e) Do not assume that a proposition is untrue because you are able to disprove the arguments that have been used to support it; there may be other, valid arguments that make it true.

Making the Paper Interesting

A mastery of the devices for attracting and holding the interest of the reader must be acquired by the writer of articles of a popular nature. These methods should be used cautiously by the writer whose purpose is to inform, rather than entertain, his fellow-workers in science. Rather let your style be characterized by unobtrusive simplicity than by inappropriate and labored ornamentation. Content is more important than style. The author should be more interested in the thing he is describing than in the words with which he describes it. Nevertheless, judicious use of some of the devices of the journalist may serve, without breach of propriety, to give a scientific paper an attractive and interesting style. These devices include:

1. Beginning with a broad introduction that gives the reader the information necessary for an understanding and appreciation of the subject. Referring to the ways in which your subject may be related to the reader's previous knowledge or experience, and suggesting benefits to be derived from further information on the subject. Emphasizing the economic or practical importance of the subject.

2. Making the paper as easy as possible for the reader to comprehend.

3. Using photographs, drawings, charts, diagrams, and curves.

4. Linking each part of the paper with some preceding part by transitional words, phrases, or sentences, so as to make a continuous story—thus sustaining the reader's interest.

5. Omitting tedious details that are not essential for accuracy and completeness; keeping the text free from repetition of data presented in tables and graphs.

6. Emphasizing the new and the unusual—the features that have "news value."

7. Preceding every dull passage by a stimulating introduction.

8. Using colorful words and vigorous turns of expression.

9. Using forcible analogies, comparisons or resemblances, similes and metaphors.

10. Introducing striking or unexpected statements, contrasts, and paradoxes.

11. Asking provocative questions.

12. Leading the reader to feel that he is doing his own thinking—not merely following; stimulating his imagination and giving him a sense of achievement.

Revising The Manuscript

After writing the first draft of your paper, begin to revise it. Revise several times, having one principal object in mind each time. Learn to rewrite between the lines. In making corrections, insertions, and transpositions, follow the methods given on pages 31 to 35. If there is not enough space between the lines for a revision, a convenient method is to write the revised passage on a slip of paper of page width and to staple this to the margin of the manuscript page. The pages need not be copied until they have become crowded with corrections.

1. Organization and Consistency. In the first revision, give attention to the order and development of the larger divisions of the paper—the sections and paragraphs. The order of the topics may need to be shifted, though this should not be necessary if a well-prepared analytical outline has been followed. If the paper is long, the first part may have to be rewritten to make it consistent with the last part. Irrelevant parts should be eliminated. Important parts may be expanded, and minor parts subordinated.

2. Sentences. In the next revision of the rough draft of the manuscript, focus attention on the sentences. Many of these may need to be revised, because they may have been written hurriedly, without much concern about details of form. Study and revise the sentences in groups, rather than singly. Make each group of sentences develop the exact ideas you wish to express. See that the members of the group stand in logical relation to one another. Achieve good organization of sentences through careful revision.

The following brief rules suggest helpful procedures: (a) Use short sentences—rarely allowing them to exceed 30 words in length. (b) Choose sentence structures that require only simple punctuation. (c) Prefer the normal order of subject, verb, and object. (d) Prefer the active voice of verbs. (e) Keep the same subject and the same voice, and use parallel structure. (f) Transpose misplaced words or phrases. (g) Insert connectives and other reference words to show relations. (h) Correct weak or vague reference of pronouns to their antecedents. (i) When advantageous, convert a loose compound sentence into a sentence with a subordinate clause.

3. Clearness. Revise sentences and paragraphs with special attention to clearness. There should be only one possible meaning, and this should be easily understood by the reader. Find the right word or phrase to convey your idea.

4. Conciseness. As a rule, the first draft of a paper should be longer and more complete than the copy that will be offered for publication. Better results are usually obtained by condensing a long paper than by expanding a short one. In shortening a paper, condense or eliminate the parts that are least needed for clearness of presentation. Strike out idle words (especially superfluous adjectives and adverbs); replace a phrase with a word; combine related sentences; eliminate repetition of an idea. Omit the obvious and the least important. Retain the essentials. Impartial counsel is valuable in aiding you to decide what is essential. In judging, put yourself in the place of the reader. It takes moral strength to "blue pencil" choice phrases, sentences, or paragraphs. But the results will justify the effort.

5. Repetition. Eliminate frequent repetition of the same sentence structure, or of the same word, particularly if close together and with different meanings.

6. Connectives. Give special attention to connectives: *and, or, similarly, but, however, nevertheless, therefore, when, where, since, because, although, if,* etc.

7. Euphony. Revise to make the article pleasing in sound when read aloud. Eliminate a succession of the same sounds, and avoid words that rhyme.

8. Punctuation. Correct the punctuation.

9. Style. Revise with special attention to consistency in the use of capitals and italics and in the style of headings. Consistency in these matters, as well as in punctuation and spelling, is essential in a manuscript prepared for the printer's use. The printer cannot depart from the rule to "follow the copy."

10. Accuracy. Read through the manuscript carefully, searching for inaccuracy or exaggeration of statement.

11. Length of Paper. A paper may need to be shortened or divided to meet the limit specified by the journal in which it is to be published. (See section on "Estimating the Length of the Printed Article," page 36.) A long paper may often be divided into two or more short papers, and these may be published separately. Care should be taken, however, to make each paper a unit, treating one central topic. If there are two or more topics in a paper, these must be the logical subdivisions of a single large topic.

Check list of some common errors in writing

A. *Inaccuracy.*

   1. Misstatement or exaggeration of fact.

   2. Misrepresentation through omission of facts.

   3. Errors in data, terms, citations.

   4. Conclusions based on faulty or insufficient evidence.

   5. Unreliable mathematical treatment.

   6. Failure to distinguish between fact and opinion.

   7. Contradictions and inconsistencies.

B. *Inadequate presentation.*

   1. Omission of important topics.

   2. Faulty order of sections or of paragraphs.

   3. Inclusion of material in wrong section or paragraph.

   4. Incomplete development of a topic.

   5. Failure to begin a section or a paragraph with a topic sentence.

   6. Weak beginning of a section or a paragraph.

   7. Inclusion of irrelevant or tedious details.

   8. Passages that are dull or hard to read.

   9. Failure to distinguish between the new and the well known.

   10. Inadequate emphasis of interpretation and conclusions.

C. *Faulty diction and style.*

   1. Long sentences (more than three or four typewritten lines) and complicated grammar.

   2. Weak sentence beginnings—a string of weak or meaningless words.

3. Lack of clearness—a sentence that requires rereading to get the meaning.

4. Long, complicated paragraphs (more than $2/3$ page of typewriting) or short, scrappy paragraphs (less than five lines of typewriting).

5. Wordiness and padding—failure to come directly to the point.

6. General words rather than definite words.

7. Dull, weak, or awkward expressions.

8. Unnecessary repetition of the same word or the same sentence structure.

9. Omission of relation words, especially in short sentences.

10. Unnecessarily technical language or too many strange words in a single sentence.

Preparing the Typewritten Copy

1. Copy for Typist. Copy for the typist should be clearly written. All of the sheets should be of the same size, preferably numbered in the upper right-hand corner.

2. One Side of Paper. Write on only one side of the paper.

3. Flat. Never roll a manuscript. If possible, keep it flat; but when necessary, it may be folded.

4. Clips. The sheets should be fastened together with clips, which can be removed easily.

5. Typewritten Manuscripts. Double-spacing must be used throughout the manuscript, including footnotes, legends, and literature citations. Exception is made only in the case of a table that must be single-spaced in order to make it fit the page.

White paper of standard size ($8^1/_2 \times 11$ inches) and ordinary weight (16 pounds) should be used.

6. Number of Copies. Three typewritten copies should usually be made. The author should retain one fully corrected copy.

7. Margins. There should be a blank space of about 2 inches above the title on the first page, 1 inch at the top of the other pages, and 1 inch at the bottom of each page. There should be a blank margin of $1^1/_4$ inches at the left side of each page and about 1 inch at the right side (but avoid dividing words at the ends of lines).

8. Page Numbers. The pages of the typewritten copy should be numbered consecutively in the upper margin, preferably in the right-hand corner.

9. Models of Style. The author should make a careful study of the journal in which his article is to be published, and he should prepare his copy so that it conforms to the best practice illustrated by current issues of the journal. Only carefully prepared, clearly typewritten manuscripts are acceptable.

10. Directions for Proofs. The author's name and the address to which proofs are to be sent should be typewritten near the top of the first page of the manuscript and enclosed in a circle.

11. Title of the Paper. The full title of the paper, including the author's name, should be typewritten 2 inches from the top of the first page of the manuscript.[4] The following example shows a complete heading that may be modified to suit the style of almost any journal.

---

4. The author's complete mail address should be printed in the paper, so that readers will know where to write for reprints; it is most convenient if given on the first page of the paper, in the heading or in a footnote to the title.

[*Example of general heading*]

INFLUENCE OF SULFONAMIDES ON GROWTH AND RESPIRATION IN BACTERIA[1]

HENRY E. MILLER AND JOHN C. STEWART

Department of Bacteriology, School of Medicine, University of Pennsylvania, Philadelphia, Pennsylvania

Received for publication [Date]

---

[1] The authors are indebted to Dr. Edward M. Johnson for helpful suggestions during the course of the study.

---

12. Tables, Footnotes, Citations, Headings, Legends. See special directions for typewriting tables (page 76), footnotes (page 56), citations (page 57), and headings (page 73).

Each individual table and each quotation exceeding five lines should be typewritten on a separate sheet of paper; these pages should be numbered consecutively with the text pages.

Footnotes should not be typewritten with the text, but should be put on separate sheets (as many footnotes as convenient being written on a sheet); these should be placed at the end of the text copy, after the literature cited. (Exception is made when preparing a manuscript for submission to certain journals. See section on "Footnotes," page 56).

The literature citations should begin on a new sheet.

The legends, or titles, of plates and figures should be written in numerical order on one or more sheets, and these should be placed after the footnotes.

13. Title for Running Headlines. A condensed title of 35 letters or less should be given by the author for the running headlines of the pages. This may be placed on a separate sheet at the end of the manuscript.

Correcting the Typewritten Copy

1. Checking. After the manuscript has been typed, the author should read the typewritten copy for errors. All tables, figures, names, quotations, and citations in the copy must be verified by comparison with the original manuscript. A convenient method of checking is to have another person slowly read aloud from the original while you follow and correct the typewritten copy.

Assume that errors are present; find and correct them. The responsibility for uncorrected errors in figures, names, citations, and quotations rests entirely with the author, since the publisher has no means of discovering such errors. It is fatal to leave them for critics to discover, after the paper has been published.

2. Indicating Special Characters. The typewritten manuscript must be clear and legible, as well as correct. Symbols, signs, superscript letters and figures, etc., must be unmistakable. For example, the symbol "Cl" (for chlorine) must be marked with a handwritten "l" above it to show that it is not "C1," since the typewriter uses the same symbol for both the letter "l" and the figure "1"; and the multiplication sign "×" must be plainly marked or the words "multiplication sign" written in the margin, to distinguish it from the letter "X". Greek letters or other unusual characters should be written clearly and, if necessary, explained by marginal notes. An ordinary dash (em dash) should be typewritten as two hyphens, without space before, between, or after them. If a hyphen occurring at the end of a typewritten line should be printed as a hyphen, mark it "=".

Corrections

1. Corrections in Body of Manuscript. If possible, write corrections in the body of the manuscript, not in the margin. If corrections are written in the margin, it may be difficult to make necessary transpositions by cutting and pasting. Do not destroy legibility by writing too many words between the lines. When it is necessary to reconstruct a long sentence or a paragraph, typewrite the revision upon a separate slip of paper of page width and paste this directly over the section rewritten. (Staples are more convenient than paste, but they should never be used in the draft sent to the printer.)

2. Corrections Horizontal. Write corrections horizontally on the page.

3. Corrections Above Line. Place the corrections in the space above the line to which they apply so that the printer will see them before he reaches the words concerned.

4. Cancellation. To cancel a word, draw a horizontal line through it. To cancel a single letter, draw a vertical line through it.

5. Restoration. To restore a word that has been canceled by mistake, rewrite the word above the one you have canceled, or make a series of dots under the word and write "Stet" in the margin.

6. Substitution. To replace one word by another, cancel the first word by drawing a horizontal line through it, and write the new word immediately above. Never write the new word directly upon the first.

7. Indicating a Paragraph. When a word should begin a new paragraph, place the "¶" sign immediately before the word.

8. Canceling a Paragraph. To cancel a paragraph division, write "No ¶" in the margin, and draw a "run-in" line from the indented word to the last of the preceding sentence.

9. Period. A period may be indicated clearly by enclosing it in a small circle.

10. Space Between Words. To separate two words that have been written together, draw a thin vertical line between them.

11. Canceling Space Between Words. To indicate that two words are to be brought together, connect them by means of half-circles above and below them. (For example: Foot ‿note.)

12. Reduction of Capital Letter. To indicate that a capital letter should be printed as a small (lower-case) letter, draw through it an oblique line sloping downward from right to left.

13. Italic Capitals. Four lines under a letter or word indicate printing in *ITALIC CAPITAL* type.

14. Capitals. Three lines under a letter or word indicate printing in ROMAN CAPITAL type.

15. Small Capitals. Two lines under a letter or word indicate printing in SMALL CAPITAL type.

16. Italics. One straight line under a letter or word indicates printing in *italic* type.

17. Boldface. One wavy line under a letter or word indicates printing in **bold-faced** type.

Insertions

1. Brief Inserts. To insert one word or a few words, write them above the line and indicate the place for their insertion by a caret (^) placed below the line.

2. Permissible Method. To insert a passage of several lines in a page of an early draft of the manuscript, the following method is convenient: Suppose the insertion is to be made in page 12 of the manuscript. Write the passage on a fresh slip of paper of page width. Mark this "Insert A in p. 12," and draw a circle around the passage. In the margin of page 12 write "Insert A," draw a circle around it, and from the circle draw a line to a caret (^) at the place where the insertion is to be made. Paste or staple this slip securely to the margin of page 12. If there are several inserts in page 12, mark these "Insert A," "Insert B," "Insert C," etc.

3. Method Generally Recommended. To insert a passage of several or many lines in a page of the manuscript, the following method is recommended: Suppose the insertion is to be made in page 7 of the manuscript. Write the passage on a fresh, full-sized sheet of paper. In the upper margin write "Insert A in p. 7," and draw a circle around the passage. Number this sheet "7A" and place it after page 7. In the margin of page 7 write "Insert A," draw a circle around it, and from the circle draw a line to a caret (^) at the place where the insertion is to be made. If there are several inserts in page 7, mark these "Insert A," "Insert B,"

"Insert C^x" (indicating the last insert by the mark ^{x}), and number the additional sheets "7A," "7B," "7C^x," placing them after page 7.

When the inserted passage is to follow the matter on a manuscript page, the sheets bearing the insert should be given interpolated page numbers—for example, "10A," "10B," "10C^X." Write at the bottom of page 10 "Follow with pages 10A, 10B, and 10C^X," and enclose this note in a circle.

Transpositions

1. Transposition by Cancellation and Insertion. The simplest way to transpose one word or a few words is to cancel them, and then write them in their new position above the line, with the place for their insertion indicated by a caret placed below the line.

2. Transposition on the Same Page. To indicate transposition of a passage to a different place on the same page, draw a circle around the passage, and from the circle draw a line to the margin and continue the line to a caret at the new place.

3. Transposition from One Page to Another. To indicate transposition of a passage to another page, the following method may be used: Suppose the passage is to be transposed from page 15 to page 14. Draw a circle around the passage on page 15, and write in the margin "tr A to p. 14." In the margin of page 14 write "tr A from p. 15," draw a circle around it, and from the circle draw a line to a caret at the desired place for the passage. Other transpositions to page 14 are designated "B," "C," etc.

Renumbering Pages

1. Consecutive Page Numbers. The methods given above refer to insertions and transpositions made in the preliminary drafts of an article.

Before the manuscript is submitted to an editor, or sent to a printer, all the material must be in proper sequence on full-sized sheets that are numbered consecutively.

2. Cutting and Pasting. Any insertions or transpositions that are necessary should be made by cutting and pasting. If smaller sheets were included with the manuscript, they might become separated and lost. The pages may be renumbered by canceling the original numbers and writing the new numbers near the canceled ones. It is not necessary to have the manuscript pages filled with typewriting; the printer will not leave a space if the lower part of a manuscript page contains no writing.

Final Revisions

1. Finished Manuscript. The author is expected to make all final revisions in the typewritten manuscript. Corrections cost nothing if they are made in the manuscript, but alterations in the proofs are very expensive and are likely to introduce inconsistencies and new errors.

2. Corrections in Manuscript. A manuscript in which there are no corrections often indicates a careless author. If the changes are not too many and are made clearly, it will not be necessary to rewrite the pages.

3. Order of Material. Before sending your manuscript to a publisher, be sure to have all parts in the proper order, as outlined below:

(a) Author's name and address to which proofs are to be sent.

(b) Title, name of author, footnote to title.

(c) Text material (each table and each long quotation being on a separate page).

(d) Literature cited (on a separate page).

(e) Footnotes (on a separate page).

(f) Legends for illustrations (on a separate page).

(g) Condensed title of 35 letters or less (on a separate page).

(h) Copy for illustrations.

Estimating the Length of the Printed Article

1. Formula and Method. An accurate estimate of the length of the text of the printed article can be made by means of the following simple formula:

Number of printed pages =

$$\frac{\text{Characters per MS line} \times \text{Lines per MS page} \times \text{Pages of MS}}{\text{Characters per printed line} \times \text{Lines per printed page}}$$

Letters, punctuation marks, and spaces between words are counted as characters; short lines at ends of paragraphs are counted as full lines.

For example, suppose that a manuscript has an average of 63 characters per line, an average of 27 lines to the page, and a length of 23 pages; and that the printed page has an average of 52 characters to the line and has 124 lines per page.

$$\text{Number of printed pages} = \frac{63 \times 27 \times 23}{52 \times 124}$$

$$= 6.1$$

Allowance must be made for the space to be occupied by tables and illustrations; this may be difficult to estimate accurately. If center headings are numerous, they should be taken into account also.

The space required for a legend may be calculated in a similar manner, by taking into account the number of characters per line of such material and the number of lines per vertical inch on the printed page.

This method of estimating the length of printed material is easier and much more accurate than any method based upon word count. Words vary in length from "a" or "if" to "nitrobenzenesulfonamides." So the number of words per line is much more variable than the number of characters. Character count is the basis of the system used by printers for copy-fitting.

2. Character Count in Typewriting. The average number of characters (including blank spaces) per manuscript line is obtained as follows: (a) Measure the length in inches of the average line on each of ten pages; (b) obtain the mean of these measurements; and (c) multiply the mean by 10 for Pica[5] typewriting or by 12 for Elite typewriting.

The average number of lines to the page is determined by a count made on a representative page.

Accurate estimation of typewritten material is facilitated by a ruler (Seneca Secretary), obtainable at stationery stores, which has scales that show directly the number of Pica or Elite characters per line and the number of lines per page.

It is sometimes desirable to typewrite a manuscript so that the average character count per line of typewriting is nearly the same as the character count per line of print. If the manuscript of the present book had been typewritten with 55 characters per line (i.e., with Pica typewritten lines $5^1/_2$ inches long), then the manuscript and printed matter would have almost matched line by line.

3. Character Count in Printing. Obtain the average number of characters per printed line as follows: (a) Count the number of characters (letters, punctuation marks, and spaces between words) in each of ten full lines picked at random in the journal in which your article is to be published; and (b) obtain the mean of these numbers.

The number of printed lines per page is determined by a count made on a full page.

Kinds Of Type

1. Roman. The light-faced, vertical type in general use is called Roman. There are three kinds of Roman type: (a) CAPITALS (caps), which may be indicated in the manuscript by drawing three lines under the word or letter to be capitalized; (b) SMALL CAPS (capital letters about half as high as caps), which may be indicated in the manuscript by drawing two lines under the letter or word; (c) lower-case letters (ordinary small letters). A diagonal line may be drawn through a capital letter to indicate that it should be printed as a small letter.

---

5. The true pica, used in measuring printed matter, is $^1/_6$ inch, not $^1/_{10}$.

2. Italics. *In italic type, or italics, the letters slope up toward the right.* To indicate italic type, draw a single straight line under the letter, word, or figure. If italic capitals are desired, underscore with four straight lines.

3. Boldface. Type with a conspicuous or heavy face is called **boldface** or **blackface**. To indicate this type, underscore with a wavy line. It should rarely be used except for headings in textbooks or for names of new species of plants and animals.

4. Typefaces or Styles of Printed Text. Computer typesetting permits today a great deal of freedom in the selection of typefaces or type styles that may be used. Among these are, for example, utopia, palatino, garamond, new century schoolbook, which are particularly suitable for text material. These type styles are often referred to as fonts. The type styles can easily be increased or reduced in size to any desired dimension through the use of computers. It can be expected that the journal, magazine, or other periodical will determine the type styles to be used.

5. Size of Type. The sizes of type are classified according to the dimensions of the bodies. When the top of the type is viewed, the height of the body indicates the size of the type, the raised character always being slightly smaller than the top of the body. The following examples illustrate the common sizes, as they appear when printed:

This line is set in 6-point type.

This line is set in 8-point type.

This line is set in 9-point type.

This line is set in 10-point type.

This line is set in 11-point type.

This line is set in 12-point type.

The unit employed in sizes of type is the point, or $1/72$ inch. Thus 10-point type has a body 10 points ($10/72$ inch) high, and has a face, or raised character, slightly less in height, so that there will be a very small space between the printed lines. When 10-point type is used in composition without additional spaces between the lines, it is said to be set "solid." Usually, however, the lines are separated by additional spaces, called leading. In most work 10-point type is set on a 12-point body, the effect being the same as if 2-point leading were inserted between the lines. The type is then said to be 10-point leaded, or, more accurately, 10-point type on 12-point body.

Scientific journals often employ 11-point type on 13-point body, with quotations set in 10-point on 12-point body; all other subsidiary matter (footnotes, legends, literature citations, tables, etc.) is usually set in 8-point type on 10-point body. This book is printed in 10-point on 12-point, with subsidiary matter in 8-point on 10-point.

6. Size of Type Page. The unit employed in measuring the width and depth of the type page is termed a pica, or a 12-point em; this term is literal, being the exact width of the capital letter "M," which is 12 points ($^{12}/_{72}$ or $^1/_6$ inch) long. Thus the type page of this book is $3^1/_2$ inches or 21 picas in width ($3^1/_2 \div {}^{12}/_{72} = 21$).

7. Spacing. The em is used as a unit for measuring printed matter. An em of 12-point type (12 set) is 12 points ($^1/_6$ inch) wide (and also 12 points high); an em of 10-point (10 set) is 10 points wide; an em of 8-point (8 set) is 8 points wide. The em and halves of the em are used for indentation and spacing, and also for expressing the lengths of dashes. An em quad is a block of type that is one em in width; the ordinary dash (—), or em dash, is the width of an em quad. An en quad is half of the width of an em, and an en dash (–), used to separate page numbers in citations, is an en in width.

8. Specifications. Complete specifications for a publication include the styles and sizes of type for body, subsidiary matter, tables, citations, headings, etc., the dimensions of the type page (in picas), the margins, the paper, the binding, instructions regarding illustrations, etc. The publisher ordinarily takes care of these details, but an editor or an author who is preparing copy ready for the printer should give considerable attention to all these questions.

CHAPTER 3

Good Form and Usage

Tenses

1. Experimental Facts. The experimental facts should be given in the *past tense*. (For example: The plants *grew* better in A than in B; the dry weight *was* greater in A than in B.)

2. Presentation. The remarks about the presentation of data should be mainly in the *present tense*. (For example: Diagrams showing yields *are* shown in figure 3. The second column of table 2 *represents* the dry weight of tops.)

3. Discussions of Results. Discussions of results may be in both the *past* and *present tenses*, swinging back and forth from the experimental facts to the presentation. (For example: The highest dry weight *is* shown for culture A, which *received* the greatest amount of the ammonium salt. This may mean that the amount of nitrogen added *was* the determining condition for these experiments.)

4. Specific Conclusions. Specific conclusions and deductions should be stated in the *past tense,* because this always emphasizes the special conditions of the particular experiments and avoids confusing special conclusions with general ones. (For example: Rice *grew* better, under the other conditions of these tests, when ammonium sulphate *was* added to the soil. Do not say: Rice *grows* better when ammonium sulphate *is* added to the soil.)

5. General Truths. When a general truth is mentioned, it should, of course, be stated in the *present tense*. Logically, a general truth is without time distinction. For example, one may say, "Many years ago, scientists were convinced that malaria *is* caused by a germ carried by a certain species of mosquito." General conclusions, well-established principles of mathematics, physics, and chemistry, should be put in the *present tense*.

Punctuation

Punctuation should follow current usage and should be uniform throughout an article. It is better to learn to apply a few simple rules than to puzzle over each case as a separate problem. The following general rules are among those most frequently applied.

1. Coordinate Statements. Put a comma before a complete statement (containing subject and predicate) introduced by *and, but, for, or, nor,* or *neither.* A semicolon or a period should be used if the statements are long or complicated.

2. Statements Introduced by Conjunctive Adverbs. Put a period or a semicolon—never a comma—before a complete statement (containing subject and predicate) introduced by *however, yet, still, nevertheless, therefore, so, hence, moreover, further, accordingly, besides, also, thus, then, indeed, otherwise.*

3. Series of Coordinate Elements. A comma should precede *and* in a series of coordinate elements such as *a, b, and c,* in which the elements may be words or phrases.

4. Adverbial Clauses. When an adverbial clause precedes its principal clause, separate the two clauses by a comma. But a comma is usually unnecessary when the adverbial clause follows. Adverbial clauses are introduced by *when, after, while, if, although, since, because, unless,* etc.

5. Relative Clauses. A non-restrictive relative clause, which is merely explanatory of an antecedent, should be set off by commas. A restrictive relative clause (omission of which would change the meaning of the sentence) should not be set off by commas. Relative clauses are generally introduced by *that, which, who,* or *whose.* Similar rules apply to non-restrictive and restrictive phrases.

6. Erroneous Junction. Use a comma to separate two parts of a sentence that might be erroneously joined in reading.

7. Interpolated Elements. Set off by commas, dashes, or parentheses an interpolated element that would make the meaning of the sentence obscure if no punctuation were used.

Capitals

The subject of capitalization is difficult to handle with definite rules, but capitals should be used according to a uniform style throughout a single article. For this reason a special revision of the manuscript should be made with the aim of making capitalization uniform.

1. Proper Nouns. Capitalize a proper noun, designating an individual person or thing. Also, capitalize a derivative of a proper noun if the derivative retains close association with the proper noun.

2. Words Derived from Proper Nouns. Be consistent in the capitalization of words derived from proper nouns. The words *volt, ampere, farad, ohm, coulomb,* and *watt* should not be capitalized. It is better to capitalize *India ink, Paris green, Prussian blue, plaster of Paris, Bordeaux mixture.*

3. Manufactured Products. Capitalize the significant parts of the name of a manufactured product. (For example: Pyrex glass, Cellophane membrane.)

4. First Words. Begin with a capital: a sentence, a complete sentence directly quoted, a legend of a table or an illustration, a center subheading, a paragraph side heading, or a topic in a table of contents.

5. Titles of Publications in Text. In the text, capitalize all important words in titles of books and periodicals and in titles of chapters in books and of articles in periodicals. (For example: Chapter XII of Clark's *The Determination of Hydrogen Ions* is entitled "Theory of the Hydrogen Electrode." An article on "Cobalt and Nickel in Soils and Plants" appeared in *Soil Science.*)

In footnote citations and in lists of literature cited, capitalize only the first word and proper nouns in English titles of books and of articles in periodicals (pages 56–64).

6. Scientific Names. In botanical and zoological work, capitalize the scientific names of genera, families, orders, classes, subdivisions, and divisions of plants and animals. (For example: *Triticum,* Gramineae, Glumiflorae, Monocotyledoneae, Angiospermae, Spermatophyta.)

7. Common Names Derived from Scientific Names. Do not capitalize common names derived from scientific names of plants and animals. (For example: ameba (amoeba) angiosperm, bacillus.)

8. Chemical and Medical Terms. Do not capitalize the names of chemicals, medicines, diseases, and anatomical parts.

9. Table, Figure, Plate. Do not capitalize *table, figure,* and *plate.* (For example: The results given in table 2 are shown as graphs in figure 3.)

10. Miscellaneous Terms. Do not capitalize such words as *plot, plat, series, class, exhibit, form, group, schedule, section, appendix, station,* etc., even when immediately followed by a figure or a capital letter.

Italics

Indicate italic type in the manuscript by drawing a single straight line under the letters, words, or numerals that are to be italicized.

1. Algebraic Symbols. Algebraic symbols and equations should be italicized. (For example: $Ax + By + C = 0$.) In equations, only the full-sized letters should be italicized; superscript and subscript letters should not be italicized. Numerals should not be italicized. (For example: $T^a + D^2 - H^b = 2L_c$.)

Chemical symbols and certain other standardized symbols are not italicized.

2. Explanatory Letters in Illustrations. Some journals prefer to use italic or slant letters to designate points, lines, objects, etc., in diagrams, drawings, and graphs. Even if Roman or vertical lettering is used in the illustration, italics should always be used in the legend and in the text when reference is made to such explanatory letters. (Example of legend of diagram: Fig. 1. Diagrammatic cross section of coconut pinna, lines AB and AC representing the two pinna wings, hinged to the midrib at A.)

3. Genera and Species. In botanical, bacteriological, zoological, and geological work, italicize scientifie names of genera, species, and varieties, and of genera alone.[6] [For example: *Phaseolus lunatus; Musa sapientum* Linn. var. *cinerea* (Blanco) Teod.; *Escherichia coli; Phytophthora.*] But do not italicize names of classes, orders, and families. When used in tables and in titles of articles, scientific names are usually not italicized.

4. Common Names Derived from Scientific Names. Do not italicize common names derived from scientific names of plants and animals. (For example: ameba (amoeba), angiosperm, bacillus, bacterium, paramecium, protozoan, streptococci.)

5. Books and Periodicals. Italicize titles of books, pamphlets, and periodicals when these appear in the text.[7] (For example: Fieser and Fieser's *Organic Chemistry*.) In footnote citations and in lists of literature cited, such titles are usually not italicized.

6. Subdivisions of Books and Periodicals. Use quotation marks—not italics—for titles of chapters in books or titles of articles in periodicals when these are given in the text. (For example: Chapter 1 of Yost and Russell's *Inorganic Chemistry* deals with "Nitrogen and Its Oxides and Sulfides." An article on "Absorption of Water by Plants" appeared in the *Botanical Review*.) In footnotes and in lists of citations, it is customary to use neither italics nor quotation marks.

7. Article. The word *the* or *a* should be italicized and capitalized when it begins the title of a book, but not when it begins the title of a periodical. (For example: Fisher's *The Design of Experiments*. An article in the *American Journal of Botany*.)

8. Technical Terms. It is permissible to italicize a letter or word to which special attention is called. An unusual technical term, requiring formal definition, may be italicized the first time it appears in an article. When an expression is regarded as quoted, it should be enclosed in quotation marks. (For example: The term *atmometric index* will be used in place of the expression "evaporating power of the air.") It is best to

---

6. Many zoological publications do not italicize scientific names. (For example: Mus musculus.)

7. Some journals use quotation marks instead of italics for titles of books.

avoid overuse of italics, capitals, and other special devices for emphasizing ideas. They often lead to an exaggeration of an idea or fact. If used excessively, they do not even give emphasis or distinction.

9. Chemical and Medical Terms. Do not italicize the names of chemicals, medicines, diseases, and anatomical parts. (For example: Uranium hexafluoride, hydroquinone, atropine, penicillin, diabetes mellitus, esophagus.)

10. Foreign Words. Do not italicize foreign words.[8] (For example: Intra-vitam staining, ceteris paribus, in medias res, in situ, en masse, e.g., i.e., viz., et al.)

Numbers

1. General. Use figures for all *definite* weights, measurements, percentages, and degrees of temperature. (For example: 6.7 kg., $2^3/_4$ inches, 15.6 ml., 112°C.) Spell out all *indefinite* and *approximate* periods of time and all other numerals that are used in a general manner. (For example: One hundred years ago, thirty years old, about two and one-half hours, ten instances, three times.) Judgment must be exercised in this matter; for instance, figures should be used in experimental data where periods of time are definite and of frequent occurrence. The conservative rule is to spell out numbers wherever possible. Some journals spell out only small numbers, those under 10 or under 100.

2. Consistency. Be consistent throughout the article in the use of figures. Do not express small numbers in words in one paragraph and in figures in another.

3. Beginning of Sentence. Never begin a sentence with a figure. Revise the sentence; or, if this is impossible, write the number in words.

4. Avoiding Confusion. Spell out numbers if confusion would be caused by the use of figures. (For example: Fifteen 200-watt Mazda lamps.)

5. References to Tables. Use figures for all numbers taken from tabular matter.

---

8. Some journals, however, italicize foreign words or phrases that have not come into common use in English.

6. Metric System. The metric system of weights and measures should usually be employed in scientific publications. Where it is customary to use a non-metric system, as in engineering, metric equivalents may be given in parentheses.

7. Abbreviations. Universally understood abbreviations of metric weights and measures may be used in tables, footnotes, and citations, and in the text when directly following figures. (For lists of abbreviations, see pages 49–55.) Non-metric units should always be spelled out, except in engineering.

8. Temperatures. Temperatures should usually be expressed in centigrade degrees. The equivalent in the Fahrenheit system may be given in parentheses if desired.

9. Time. Employ figures for hours of the day, using a colon to separate hours and minutes. (For example: 7:00 a.m.; 3:30 p.m.; 12 m.; 12 p.m.)

10. Dates. Use figures for days of the month, spelling out the name of the month and omitting *d, th, st.* (For example: September 21, 1946.)

11. Money. Use figures for sums of money written with a dollar sign. (For example: $15.65; $25, *not* $25.00; but definite precision sometimes requires the use of ciphers at right of decimal.)

12. Twenty-one to Ninety-nine. Cardinal numbers from twenty-one to ninety-nine, inclusive, should be written with hyphens.

13. Hyphens in Ordinal Numbers. Ordinal numbers should be joined with hyphens. (For example: Thirty-fourth, one-hundred-and-eleventh.)

14. Comma in Figures. In tabular matter, use a comma to separate a number of four or more figures, grouping three units to the right. In the text, omit a comma in a number containing four figures.

15. Fractions. Decimal fractions should be employed in the metric system. Common fractions used in an indefinite manner should be spelled out, joining the numerator to the denominator with a hyphen. (For example: One-half of the balance, two-thirds of the residue, about one-tenth of this quantity.) Use figures for common fractions when designating definite weights and measurements. (For example: $^1/_2$-in. pipe.) Simple fractional expressions may be written with a slant line. Fractions that would require very large numbers in numerator or denominator should be expressed decimally. Very small fractions are conveniently indicated by means of negative exponents. (For example: $7.5 \yen 10^{-8}$.)

16. Half and Quarter. Compounds of *half* and *quarter* should be written with a hyphen. (For example: Half-full; quarter-past. But: One half was dried; the other was not.)

17. Per Cent. Omission of a period after *per cent* is favored by most writers. (Some journals use the symbol % in tables or even in the text.)

18. Per cent and Percentage. Do not use *per cent* for *percentage.* *Per cent* should be preceded by a number. (For example: Three analyses gave the following percentages of sugar: 93.2, 93.1, and 92.9. There was an increase of 15 per cent in production.)

19. Basis for Percentage. If there is possibility of misunderstanding, make clear the basis used for expressing percentages. (For example: The phrase "a 5 per cent solution of alcohol in water" correctly means 5 grams of alcohol in 100 grams of the solution, but some writers use it to mean 5 ml. of alcohol in 100 ml. of the solution. Also, in reporting analyses of foods, plant and animal tissues, blood, milk, etc., it is essential to specify whether moisture-free weight, fresh weight, or volume is used as the basis for percentages.)

20. Standard Error or Probable Error. Be careful to state whether *standard error* or *probable error* is meant in an expression such as "10.3 ± 0.2 grams."

21. Plural. Use the plural form when referring to a quantity or measurement of more than one. (For example: About one and one-half kilometers; $1^1/_4$ inches.)

22. Singular and Plural Forms of Verbs. When total quantity is indicated, the singular verb may be used. (For example, it is permissible to write: To each culture 300 ml. of solution was added.) But it is better to recast the sentence and avoid the difficulty. (For example: Each culture received 300 ml. of solution.)

23. Mathematical Expressions. To simplify printing, reduce mathematical expressions to a single line when possible. Use a slant line to signify division, and use fractional exponents instead of square-root and cube-root signs.

24. Verification. The use of statistical or mathematical formulas should be checked by a specialist in the field.

25. Significant Figures. In publishing a computed number, retain no more significant digits than are consistent with its accuracy. In statistical work the following rule may be a useful guide: In the published constant, retain no figures beyond the position of the first significant figure in one-third the standard error; in all computations, keep two more places. (For example: 129 ± 3, *not* 129.2 ± 3.1.)

26. Roman Numerals. Where possible, avoid the use of Roman numerals, since they are not readily understood.

Abbreviations of Units of Weight and Measure

The general rule regarding abbreviations is to employ only those abbreviations which you know are used by careful writers in your science, and to conform to the style of the publication in which your article is to appear. The names of chemical compounds, rather than their symbols, should be used in the text. It is a good rule always to spell out the names of units of weights and measurements of all systems except the metric; the metric abbreviations are understood in all parts of the world.[9] This rule is often ignored, however, where brevity is essential.

In medical work, "gram" and "grain" should always be spelled out, because errors are likely to result from the use of such abbreviations as "g.," "gm.," "gr.," and "grs.," and misinterpretation of such an abbreviation can lead to serious harm.

---

9. For the sake of economy, the *Journal of the American Chemical Society* uses the abbreviations %, °A., cm., cc., ml., g., Å., m. p., f. p., b. p., cal., and kcal. rather than the words.

A Set of Standard Abbreviations

Standard abbreviations of units of weight and measure are given in the accompanying table.

The following general principles should be observed:

1. Period. In accordance with conservative practice, a period is used after each abbreviation, although it is omitted after certain symbols.[10]

2. Singular and Plural. The same form is used for both singular and plural. (For example: 0.5 kg., 12.3 kg.)

3. Small Letters. Small letters are used for abbreviations; but some symbols are capitalized.

Most common units of weight and measure and their abbreviations

UNIT	ABBREVIATION
Ångstrom	Å
are	a.
barrel	bbl.
board foot	bd. ft.
bushel	bu.
carat, metric	c.
centare	ca.
centigram	cgm.
centiliter	cl.
centimeter	cm.
chain	ch.
cubic centimeter (milliliter)	cc.
cubic centimeter	cu. cm.
cubic decimeter	cu. dm.
cubic dekameter	cu. dkm.
cubic foot	cu. ft.
cubic hectometer	cu. hm.

---

10. The Government Printing Office and many journals omit the period after the abbreviations of metric units. For example: mm, kv, °C; but a. c., d. c., e. m. f. The trend is toward the omission of the period.

UNIT	ABBREVIATION
cubic inch	cu. in.
cubic kilometer	cu. km.
cubic meter	cu. m.
cubic mile	cu. mi.
cubic millimeter	cu. mm.
cubic yard	cu. yd.
curies	spell out
decigram	dg.
deciliter	dl.
decimeter	dm.
decistere	ds.
dekagram	dkg.
dekaliter	dkl.
dekameter	dkm.
dekastere	dks.
dram	dr.
dram, apothecaries'	dr. ap.
dram, avoirdupois	dr. av.
dram, fluid	fl. dr.
fathom	fath.
foot	ft.
firkin	fir.
furlong	fur.
gallon	gal.
grain	gr.—but spell out in medical work
gram	g., gm.—but spell out in medical work
hectare	ha.
hectogram	hg.
hectoliter	hl.
hectometer	hm.
hogshead	hhd.
hundredweight	cwt.

Most common units of weight and measure and their abbreviations
(Continued)

UNIT	ABBREVIATION
inch	in.
kilogram	kg.
kiloliter	kl.
kilometer	km.
link	li.
liquid	liq.
liter	l.
meter	m.
metric ton	t.
microgram (0.001 mgm.)	μg, γ
micromicron (not millimicron)	μμ
micron	μ
mile	mi.
millicuries	spell out
milligram	mg.
milliliter	ml.
millimeter	mm.
millimicron	mμ
minim	min.
ounce	oz.
ounce, apothecaries'	oz. ap.
ounce, avoirdupois	oz. av.
ounce, fluid	fl. oz.
ounce, troy	oz. t.
peck	pk.
pennyweight	dwt.
pint	pt.
pound	lb.
pound, apothecaries'	lb. ap.
pound, avoirdupois	lb. av.
pound, troy	lb. t.
quart	qt.
rod	rd.
roentgen	r.

Most common units of weight and measure and their abbreviations
(Concluded)

UNIT	ABBREVIATION
scruple, apothecaries'	sq. ap.
square centimeter	sq. cm.
square chain	sq. ch.
square decimeter	sq. dm.
square dekameter	sq. dkm.
square foot	sq. ft.
square hectometer	sq. hm.
square inch	sq. in.
square kilometer	sq. km.
square meter	sq. m.
square mile	sq. mi.
square millimeter	sq. mm.
square rod	sq. rd.
square yard	sq. yd.
stere	s.
troy	t.
yard	yd.

The Greek Alphabet

A	α	Alpha	I	ι	Iota	P	ρ	Rho
B	β	Beta	K	κ	Kappa	Σ	σ	Sigma
Γ	γ	Gamma	Λ	λ	Lambda	T	τ	Tau
Δ	δ	Delta	M	μ	Mu	Y	υ	Upsilon
E	ε	Epsilon	N	ν	Nu	Φ	φ	Phi
Z	ζ	Zeta	Ξ	ξ	Xi	X	χ	Chi
H	η	Eta	O	ο	Omicron	Ψ	ψ	Psi
Θ	θ	Theta	Π	π	Pi	Ω	ω	Omega

Abbreviations Used in Engineering

The following list shows abbreviations used in many engineering publications.

TERM	ABBREVIATION
alternating current	spell out, or a-c. when used as compound adjective
amperes	spell out
boiler horse power	boiler h.p.
brake horse power	b.h.p.
British thermal units	B.t.u.
candle power	c.p.
centigrade	cent.
centimeters	cm.
circular mils	cir. mils
counter electromotive force	counter e.m.f.
cubic	cu.
diameter	spell out
direct current	spell out, or d-c. when used as compound adjective
electric horse power	e.h.p.
electromotive force	e.m.f.
Fahrenheit	Fahr.
feet	ft.
foot-pounds	ft-lb.
gallons	gal.
grains	gr.
gram-calories	g-cal.
grams	g., gm.
high-pressure cylinder	spell out
hours	hr.
inches	in.
indicated horse power	i.h.p.

TERM	ABBREVIATION
kilogram-calories	kg-cal.
kilogram-meters	kg-m.
kilograms	kg.
kilometers	km.
kilovolts	kv.
kilovolt-amperes	kv-a.
kilowatt-hours	kw-hr.
kilowatts	kw.
magnetomotive force	m.m.f.
mean effective pressure	spell out
megacycle	spell out
meter-kilograms	m-kg.
meters	m.
microfarad	spell out
microwave	spell out
miles	mi.
miles per hour per second	mi. per hr. per sec.
milligrams	mg.
millimeters	mm.
minutes	min.
ohms	spell out
per	spell out
percentage	per cent (or % in tabular matter)
pounds	lb.
power-factor	spell out
revolutions per minute	rev. per min. (or r.p.m. in tabular matter)
seconds	sec.
square	sq.
square -root-of-mean-square	r.m.s.
ton-mile	spell out
tons	spell out
volt-amperes	spell out

54

TERM	ABBREVIATION
volts	spell out
watt-hours	watt-hr.
watts	spell out
watts per candle power	watts per c.p.
yards	yd.

Names of Plants and Animals

Plants

1. Complete Name. A complete plant name should include the name of the genus (in italics), the name of the species (in italics), and the abbreviated designation of the person who named the plant (in Roman type). (For example: *Oryza sativa* Linn.) It is often desirable to add the common name of the plant, and in some cases the name of the family (both in Roman type). [For example: *Shorea polysperma* Merr. (tanguile), Dipterocarpaceae; *Hemileia vastatrix* Berk. and Br. (coffee rust), Pucciniaceae.]

Unfortunately, a plant may have received several common and scientific names. Where scientific names differ in standard or commonly used works, one is chosen and the others are treated as synonyms. If a synonym is much used, it is customary to insert it in parentheses after the accepted name. In an index, accepted names are usually printed in Roman type, and synonyms in italics. In tables and in titles, names of genera and species are usually printed in Roman type.

2. Necessity of Scientific Name. The scientific name, in addition to the common name, should be given when the plant is first mentioned in a paper. Use names that will be understood by foreign readers, many of whom must translate an article before they can understand it. For example, *Manihot utilissima is* universally understood by botanists; but the common name camoteng cahoy would be unintelligible to readers in many parts of the world. The scientific name may be enclosed in parentheses after the common name. [For example: The experiments described in this paper deal with the growth of rice (*Oryza sativa* Linn.).]

3. Use of Common Name. In papers dealing with agriculture, the scientific name of a well-known plant need not be repeated; after the scientific name has been given once, the plant may be referred to by its common name in the rest of the paper.

4. Capitalization. The generic name should be capitalized, and the specific name usually should not be capitalized.[11] There is good authority, however, for capitalizing names of species derived from generic names, or from names of persons. (For example: *Acer Negundo, Ustilago Zeae, Magnolia Soulangeana.*)

5. Variety Name. Capitalize the vernacular names of plant varieties (Yellow Dent corn, Binocol rice, Carabao mango, New Era cowpeas), but not the latinized names of varieties (*Lathyrus palustris* Linn. var. *linearifolius* Ser.).

Animals

1. Complete Name. In papers on zoology or one of its branches, such as entomology, names of animals should be given in a form similar to that used for plant names. [For example: *Agromyza destructor* Malloch (bean fly), Family Agromyzidae, Order Diptera; *Bubalus bubalis* Lyd. (carabao), Bovidae; *Equus caballus* Linn. (horse) Equidae.][12]

2. Use of Common Name. Well-known kinds of animals may be referred to by their common names; the complete scientific name may be given only at the beginning of the paper, or it may be omitted entirely. (For example: Berkshire swine, Hereford cattle, horse, Barred Plymouth Rock fowls.)

Footnotes

1. Reference Numbers in Text. Footnotes pertaining to the text should be numbered consecutively (from 1 up) throughout each article and indicated by superscript numerals ([1, 2, 3,] etc.). The reference numeral to the footnote should be placed in the text after the word or sentence to which the footnote refers. It is placed *after* a punctuation mark if one

---

11. The Government Printing Office never capitalizes the specific name. (For example: *Ustilago zeae.*)

12. Many zoological publications do not italicize scientific names.

occurs. Indicate the superscript numeral by typewriting it above the line and placing a V-shaped mark under it. Observe that these references apply to the text only; tabulations employ a separate series of symbols or superscript letters for each table. If mathematical formulas containing exponents appear in the text, care should be taken to avoid confusing exponents and footnote reference numbers.

2. Footnotes at End of Manuscript. Footnotes should not be in the body of the text; the text should have the reference numbers only. Footnotes should be typewritten double-spaced on one or more separate sheets (as many footnotes to a sheet as convenient). Each footnote should be indented as a paragraph, and should be preceded by a superscript numeral corresponding to the reference number in the body of the manuscript. The sheets bearing footnotes should be put at the end of the text copy, each sheet bearing the word "Footnotes," enclosed in a circle.

This method is necessary in order to facilitate composition on the typesetting machines. When printed, each footnote will be inserted at the foot of the proper page.

Exception is made when a manuscript is being prepared for submission to a journal which requires that the footnotes be placed in the text of the manuscript. In this case each footnote is inserted as a separate line, or lines, immediately following the line of text containing the reference numeral, and the footnote is set off by short rules from the text material above and below it.

3. Misuse of Footnotes. Use footnotes only where they are indispensable. Include important material in the text; omit irrelevant material.

Literature Citations

Citations to literature are given in a list at the end of the paper or in footnotes distributed throughout the paper. The method of handling text references to citations and of printing the citations differs in detail in the various scientific journals. A uniform standard, though highly desirable, has not been adopted by editors and publishers. It may be noted, however, that there is a modern trend toward simplification and away from the use of small capitals, italics, and superscript and black-faced numerals, all of which make extra work for author, typist, editor, and printer.

1. Making a Card File. In writing citations in the library, follow the exact style employed by the journal in which you expect to have the paper published, and take time to check every item. Include the full title for your own use, even if it will be eliminated in publication. Put only one citation on a card. Small cards (3 by 5 inches) are more convenient to handle, but large cards (5 by 8 inches) have the advantage of providing plenty of space for an abstract of the article. To permit revisions, it is best to keep the citations in the form of a card file until the rest of the manuscript is ready for the final typing. Then they are typewritten from the cards on sheets of manuscript paper.

2. Verifying the Citations. Verify each item in every citation by going to the library or the reprint file and looking up all the publications. Many errors result from failure to check citations taken from literature lists. As each citation is checked, make a clear notation on the card, so that doubt will not arise later. You must assume full responsibility for the accuracy and completeness of your citations. Although the editor may make minor revisions in the form of the citations to suit the style of his journal, he cannot be expected to correct spelling, figures, etc., nor supply missing data.

3. The Heading. When the citations are printed at the end of the paper, the heading "Literature cited" (or "References") is usually employed. Only those citations which are specifically referred to in the text are included in such a list. It is customary to use the heading "Bibliography" only in books or articles of a general or popular nature, where specific reference to all the citations is not made in the text.

4. Directions for Two Methods. Directions are given below for two methods of handling citations. Each is widely used in scientific literature. The first method has the following advantages not possessed by the second: (1) Reference by author and year of publication gives the reader the information he wants in the text and enables him to locate the citation easily in the alphabetical list at the end of the paper, or to use the list independently as a source of literature. This method of reference is most convenient for the author because it allows him to add or delete citations during the revisions of the manuscript, without the necessity of repeatedly renumbering the series. (2) The citations are printed in a form that avoids the use of troublesome black-faced and italic types. A colon after the volume number clearly separates it from the page numbers that follow.

First Method

1. Text Reference to Citation. Reference to a citation is made by means of the author's name followed by the year of publication in parentheses. [For example: Foster (1995).] If the paper that is cited has more than two authors, reference may be made by adding "et al." to the name of the first. [For example: Smith et al. (1996).] Where the author's name does not form a part of a sentence in the text, reference is made in parentheses after the proper word or at the end of the sentence. If reference is made to several papers published in the same year by one author, the suffixes a, b, c, etc., are used after the year number, the suffixes being chosen according to the order of reference in the text.[13]

2. Arrangement of Citations. The citations are typewritten, double-spaced throughout, from the card file. They begin on a new sheet of paper, at the end of the article, bearing the center heading "Literature cited," in capitals.

The citations are arranged alphabetically according to authors' names. The author's name is typewritten flush with the left-hand edge of the writing, and second and succeeding lines are indented five spaces on the typewriter. A number of papers by the same author are listed in chronological order, according to the year of publication; several papers in one year are given the suffixes a, b, c, etc., after the year number; a long dash is used in place of repetition of the author's name. In case of multiple authorship, the name of the first author usually determines the alphabetical and chronological order in the list.

---

13. Where greater brevity is required, reference to citations is made in the text by numerals in parentheses. The numeral is placed after the author's name, or after the proper word or at the end of the sentence. To shorten the text, the names of many of the authors are omitted. The numerals in the text refer to citations at the end of the article, which are numbered in the order of text reference, or preferably alphabetized and then numbered.

In the early drafts of the manuscript, it is advantageous to use the author's name and the year of publication as the reference in the text. Just before the final typing, the cards are numbered serially and the text references are changed to numerals, as described above.

Journals with numbered volumes

3. Items and Form. Each citation of a paper in a journal includes the following items:

(a) *Surname of author* followed by a comma and initials, in large and small caps. (Underscore with two lines to indicate the small caps.) (For example: WILLIAMS, R. R.) If there are several authors, only the name of the first is inverted. (For example: GARNER, W. W., AND H. A. ALLARD.)

(b) *Year of publication* followed by a period. (For example: 1996. If several papers published in the same year by one author are cited, the year number is followed by a, b, c, etc., in the order of reference in the text. (For example: 1996a, 1996b, 1996c.)

(c) *Title of paper,* exactly like the original in wording and punctuation. A period follows the title. Only proper names are capitalized, except in Danish, Dutch, or German. (If extreme brevity is required in the citation, the title of the paper is omitted.)

(d) *Abbreviated name of serial publication* in the approved form. (See section on "Abbreviations of Periodical Publications," page 70.)

(e) *Volume number* followed by a colon.

(f) *Page numbers.* The number of the first page of the paper is separated by an en dash (indicated by a hyphen) from the number of the last page, and the latter is followed by a period.

> HASTINGS, J.W. 1996. Chemistries and colors of bioluminescent reactions: A review. Gene. 173: 5–11.

> MAIA, I.G., HAENNI, A.-L., AND BERNARDI, F. 1996. Potyviral H-C–Pro: A multifunctional protein. Jour. Gen. Vir. 77: 1335–1341.

> MODEL, MICHAEL A., AND OMANN, GENEVA M. 1996. Cell Polarization as a Possible Mechanism of Response Termination. Biochem. and Biophys. Res. Com. 224: 516–521.

MOYER, LINDA, WARWICK, MARIAN, AND MAHONEY, FRANCIS. 1996. Prevention of Hepatitis A Virus Infection. Amer. Fam. Phys. 54: 107–116.

RIEGER, DONALD. 1996. Embryo Biotechnology for the Canadiean Dairy Industry. Agri-food Res. Ont. 19: 30–31.

SMITH, R.W., AND KUDSK, K. 1996. Surgical and Nutritional Nightmares: What Do We Do Now? Amer. Fam. Phys. 11: 66–68.

Books

4. Items and Form. The copyright date is used as the year of publication. The following examples illustrate the form used:

FERREL, R. Medical Physiology. 9th ed. 804 p. Philadelphia: W.B. Saunders.

HAKKO, K. 1996. List of cultures: microorganisms. 10th ed. 521 p. Osaka: The Institute for Fermentation.

JUNGKIND, D. L. 1995. Antimicrobial resistance: a crisis in health care. 367 p. New York: Plenum Press.

NORDLING, C. 1996. X-rays in natural science and medicine. 474 p. Stockholm: Royal Swedish Academy of Sciences.

Yearbooks

5. Items and Form. An example illustrates the form used:

MATTHEWS, A. F. 1996. Metals and Minerals. Minerals Yearbook 1994: 1205–1231.

Yearbooks are not numbered as volumes, but only by years. The actual time of publication—as shown in the example—is usually one or two years later than the period covered by the yearbook.

Experiment station bulletins

6. Items and Form. In citing experiment station bulletins and other issues of serial publications bearing an individual number but no volume number, the following form is used:

> BEATH, O. A., H. F. EPPSON, AND C. S. GILBERT. 1996. Selenium and other toxic minerals in soils and vegetation. Wyoming Agric. Exper. Sta. Bull. no. 206: 1–55.

Second Method

1. Text Reference to Footnote Citations. The citations are given as footnotes, numbered consecutively (from 1 up) throughout the paper (in the order in which they are given in the text) and indicated in the text by superscript numerals. If other footnotes occur (except those in tables), they are numbered 1 in the same series with the citations. A repeated reference is given the number of the original reference. The superscript reference numeral to each footnote is placed in the text after the word or sentence to which the footnote refers; it is put after a punctuation mark if there is one. The superscript numeral is indicated by typewriting it above the line and putting a V-shaped mark under the numeral.

2. Footnotes. The footnotes are not inserted in the text, but are typewritten double-spaced on separate sheets (as many as convenient on a sheet). Each footnote is indented as a paragraph and is preceded by a full-sized numeral in parentheses corresponding to the reference number in the text.[14] The sheets bearing footnotes are put at the end of the text copy, each sheet marked with the word "Footnotes," enclosed in a circle.

Journals with numbered volumes

3. Items and Form. Each citation of a paper in a journal includes the following items:

(a) *Footnote reference number* in parentheses.

---

14. Superscript numerals are used in some journals for both text references and footnotes.

In some journals, full-sized numerals in parentheses in the text refer to citations at the end of the article, which are numbered in the order of text references or are alphabetized and then numbered.

(b) *Initials and surname of author* followed by a comma, in large and small caps (latter indicated by underscoring with two lines). (Some journals use ordinary lower-case letters, not small caps.)

(c) *Abbreviated name of serial publication* in italic type (indicated by underlining with a single straight line), followed by a comma. (Some journals use Roman, not italic.)

See section on "Abbreviations of periodical publications," page 68. Note also that the journals published by the American Chemical Society use the abbreviations given by *Chemical Abstracts* in its "List of Periodicals Abstracted."

(d) *Volume number* followed by a comma, both in black-faced type (indicated by underlining with a wavy line).

(e) *Number of the page cited*—that of the first page of the article.

(f) *Year of publication of the article,* in parentheses, followed by a period.

(1) DAVID R. CARRIER, *Phys. Zoo.*, **69**, 467 (1996).

(2) L. ZHANG, *Polymer Jour.*, **28**, 471 (1996).

(3) STEPHEN S. HECHT, *Preventive Med.*, **25**, 7 (1996).

(4) JOSEPH H. MANSON, *Primates*, **37**, 145 (1996).

(5) RONALD L. DAVIS, *Phys. Rev.*, **43**, 214 (1996).

Simplified form

Only one style of type is required in the following form:

D. H. Sloan, Phys. Rev. 43:214 (1993).

Books

4. Items and Form. In citing books, the form shown by the following examples is used:

W. LUDWIG, "Symmetries in Physics: Group Theory Applied to Physical Problems," Springer, New York, 1996, p. 201.

TADAHISA FUNAKI, "Nonlinear Stochastic PDE's: Hydrodynamic Limit and Burger's Turbulence," Springer, New York, 1996, p. 133.

ROBERT J. ADLER, "Stochastic Modelling in Physical Oceanography," Birkhauser, Boston, 1996, pp. 475, 483.

LAURA K. SMITH, "Brunstrom's Clinical Kinesiology," F.A. Davis, Philadelphia, 1996, pp. 31, 44.

Yearbooks

5. Items and Form. The following example illustrates the form used:

N. B. MELCHER, *Minerals Yearbook,* 1996, 751 (1988).

Experiment station bulletins

6. Items and Form. In citing experiment station bulletins and other issues of serial publications bearing an individual number but no volume number, the form shown by the following example is used.

H. B. VICKERY AND G. W. PUCHER, *Conn. Agric. Exper. Sta. Bull.,* 352 (1996).

Abbreviations of Periodical Publications

In preparing literature citations, the author should base abbreviations of serials upon a careful study of those used by the publication in which his paper is to be printed. Capitalization, in particular, varies in different journals. A uniform style must be used throughout a single bibliography.

The rules given below are intended to make it as easy as possible for the readers of your article to look up the literature references in the library.

1. Beginning with Key Word in Library List. The abbreviated name of a periodical publication should always begin with the key word under which the name is entered alphabetically in all library lists.

(a) "A serial not published by a society or a public office is entered under the first word, not an article *[a, an, the,* or equivalent], of the latest form of the title."

Annual Review of Biochemistry .... Ann. Rev. Bio-chem.
Annalen der Physik .... Ann. d. Physik
The Botanical Review .... Bot. Rev.
The Journal of Experimental Biology .... Jour. Exper. Biol.

(b) "A serial published by a society, but having a distinctive title, is entered under the title, with reference from the name of the society."

American Journal of Botany (published by
   the Botanical Society of America) .... Amer. Jour. Bot.
Chemical and Engineering News (published
   by the American Chemical Society) .... Chem. And Engineer.
                                     News
Science (published by the American Association for the Advancement of Science) .... Science

(c) "The journals, transactions, proceedings, etc., of a society are entered under the first word, not an article, of the latest form of the name of the society."

This rule applies to publications of a *society,* an *association,* an *academy,* an *institution,* or a *university.*

If the name of the society (or other organization) *is put at the beginning* of the abbreviated title of such a publication, the reader will naturally look under that name in the library card catalogue, and so will easily find the publication. If, on the contrary, the word "Bull.," "Jour.," "Proc.," or "Trans.," is placed at the beginning of the abbreviated title, the reader is likely to waste much time searching in the library catalogue under that word.

If all authors and editors would adopt this library rule and adhere to it consistently, they would save their readers much loss of time.

Academie des Sciences, Paris.
   Comptes Rendus .... Acad. des Sci. Paris,
                                     Compt. Rend.

American Medical Association.
Journal .... Amer. Med. Assoc.,
Jour.

Cambridge Philosophical Society.
Proceedings .... Cambridge Philosoph.
Soc., Proc.

Deutsche Chemische Gesellschaft.
Berichte .... Deut. Chem. Gesell-
sch., Ber.

National Academy of Sciences.
Proceedings .... Nat. Acad. Sci., Proc.

Torrey Botanical Club.
Bulletin .... Torrey Bot. Club, Bull.

U. S. Bureau of Standards.
Bulletin .... U. S. Bur. Standards,
Bull.

U. S. Bureau of Standards.
Journal of Research .... U. S. Bur. Standards,
Jour. Res.

U. S. Bureau of Standards.
Technical Papers .... U. S. Bur. Standards,
Tech. Papers

(d) "Learned societies and academies of Europe, other than English, with names beginning with an adjective denoting royal privilege are entered under the first word following the adjective. These adjectives, Kaiserlich, Königlich, Reale, Imperiale, etc., are abbreviated to K., R., I., etc., and are disregarded in the arrangement."

(e) "Colleges and universities having a geographical designation are entered under the name of the city, state, or country contained in the title."

(f) "Observatories, botanical and zoological gardens, etc., not having a distinctive name, are entered under the name of the place in which they are located, unless they are affiliated with a university, in which case they are entered under the name of the university."

2. Using the Original Language. The vernacular should be used, not a translation. Just as one looks for a book by Felix Klein under *Klein,* not under *Small* or *Little,* so must one look for the Polish academy under its Polish name and use it in printed citations even though one cannot pronounce it.

> *Use* Lund. Observ. Meddel.; *not* Contributions of the Observatory of Lund.

> *Do not use* Acad. *for* Akad. *or* Accad.

3. Avoiding Extreme Brevity. Abbreviation of words—particularly of the first word—should not be carried too far.

In such cases as "Ann.," "Biol.," or "Geol.," when this is the first word, either the rest of the title should be written so as to leave no doubt as to the language of the title, or else the first word should be written in full. "Anales," "Annalen," "Annals," and "Annual" are far apart in a large catalogue. "Ann. d. Phys." might be either French or German.

> *Use* Amer. Chem. Soc., Jour.; *not* J. A. C. S.

> *Use* Arch. f. Tech. Mess.; *not* A. T. M.

> *Use* Optic. Soc. Amer., Jour.; *not* J. O. S. A.

4. Including All Important Words. All important words should usually be included in the abbreviated title.

Abbreviations in code form are permissible if the readers understand that a key is readily available in the library. For example, the readers learn that the abbreviations consisting only of "Ber.," "Ann.," "Compt. Rend.," etc., in the journals published by the American Chemical Society can be deciphered by means of the key given by *Chemical Abstracts* in its "List of Periodicals Abstracted."

5. Omitting Articles and Prepositions. Articles and prepositions may be omitted when their omission does not lead to obscurity.

But use Soc. de Biol., *not* Soc. Biol., *for* Société de Biologie, *to avoid confusion with* Société Biologique.

6. Names of Places and Persons. Names of places and persons should not be abbreviated.

Cambridge Philosoph. Soc., Proc.

Franklin Inst., Jour.

Liebig's Ann. d. Chem.

Inst. Pasteur, Bull.

But note that Amer. (for American), Brit. (for British), Deut. (for Deutsche), and U. S. (for United States) are commonly accepted.

7. Editor's Name. An editor's name should be avoided unless it is in the official title.

> *Use* Ann. d. Physik, ser. 2, *or* Ann. d. Physik [2]; *not* Poggendorff's Annalen.

> *But* Pflüger's Archiv *is correct.*

8. Part, Section, or Division. When publications of an institution are organized in parts, the section or division designation should be included.

> Preuss. Akad. d. Wissens., Phys.-Math. Kl., Sitz. Ber.

> Akad. d. Wissens., Wien, Sitz. Ber. 2A

9. Series Number. The series number should always be given, in addition to the volume number and year number, in case the set is numbered in series.

> Philosoph. Mag., ser. 7, *or* Philosoph. Mag. [7].

10. List of Abbreviations. The following list shows some common abbreviations of words in the names of periodical publications:

Abstracts	Absts.	Anthropological	Anthropol.
Academy	Acad.	Anzeiger	Anz.
Agricultural	Agric.	Association	Assoc.
American	Amer.	Archiv	Arch.
Anales	Ann.	Archives	Arch.
Analytical	Analyt.	Archivio	Arch.
Anatomical	Anat.	Astronomical	Astron.
Annalen	Ann.		
Annals	Ann.	Bacteriology	Bacteriol.
Annual	Ann.	Bakteriologie	Bakteriol.

Beiträge	Beitr.	Gazette	Gaz.
Berichte	Ber.	Gazzetta	Gazz.
Biochemical	Biochem.	General	Gen.
Biological	Biol.	Genetics	Genet.
Biologie	Biol.	Geographical	Geogr.
Biologique	Biol.	Geological	Geol.
Botanical	Bot.	Geologische	Geol.
Botanik	Bot.	Gesellschaft	Gesellsch.
Botanisches	Bot.		
Botany	Bot.	History	Hist.
British	Brit.		
Bulletin	Bull.	Industry	Indus.
Bureau	Bur.	Institute	Inst.
		International	Internat.
Centralblatt	Centralbl.		
Chemical	Chem.	Jahrbuch	Jahrb.
Chemie	Chemie	Jahresbericht	Jahresb.
Chemistry	Chem.	Journal	Jour.
Chimie	Chimie		
Clinical	Clin.	Magazine	Mag.
Comptes	Compt.	Mathematics	Math.
Contributions	Contr.	Mechanical	Mech.
		Medical	Med.
der	d.	Medicine	Med.
Deutsche	Deut.	Monographs	Monogr.
Diseases	Dis.	Monthly	Month.
		Morphologisches	Morphol.
Ecology	Ecol.	Morphology	Morphol.
Economics	Econ.		
Edition	Ed.	National	Nat.
Electric	Elec.	Natural	Nat.
Engineering	Engineer.	Neurology	Neurol.
Ergebnisse	Ergebn.		
Ethnology	Ethnol.	Paleontologie	Paleontol.
Experiment	Exper.	Palentology	Paleontol.
Experimental	Exper.	Pathology	Pathol.
Experimentale	Exper.	Pharmacology	Pharmacol.
		Philosophical	Philosoph.
für	f.	Physical	Phys.

69

Physik	Physik	Scienze	Sci.
Physikalische	Physikal.	Service	Serv.
Physiological	Physiol.	Society	Soc.
Physique	Physique	Station	Sta.
Political	Polit.	Surgery	Surg.
Proceedings	Proc.	Survey	Surv.
Protistenkunde	Protistenk.		
Psychological	Psychol.	Technology	Technol.
Psychology	Psychol.	Therapeutics	Therap.
Publication	Pub.	Transactions	Trans.
		Tropical	Trop.
Quarterly	Quart.		
		United States	U. S.
Record	Rec.	und	u.
Rendus	Rend.		
Report	Rept.	Verhandlungen	Verhandl.
Research	Res.		
Review	Rev.	Zeitschrift	Ztschr.
Revue	Rev.	Zeitung	Ztg.
Rivista	Riv.	Zentralblatt	Zentralbl.
Royal	Roy.	Zoologie	Zool.
		Zoologischer	Zool.
Science	Sci.	Zoology	Zool.
Scientific	Scient.		

Abstracts and Quotations

Abstracts

1. Form. Reference to a cited publication should usually be made in the form of an indirect quotation or a brief abstract that summarizes the discussion presented in the original publication.

2. Credit. Always give credit for ideas taken directly from any publication.

3. Citation. A citation of each article mentioned must appear in your literature cited or in a footnote.

4. Punctuation. Indirect quotations should not be enclosed in quotation marks.

Quotations

1. Permissions. Written permission must be obtained from the copyright owner before printing or otherwise reproducing material from a copyrighted publication.

2. Form. When direct quotations are needed, they should be enclosed in quotation marks, and should reproduce the exact words of the original publication, including all details of spelling, capitalization, and punctuation. Corrections or remarks inserted by the one who quotes must be placed in square brackets [ ]. Omissions must be indicated by a series of four periods. The author should carefully compare the typewritten copy with the original printed matter; this should be done each time the manuscript is copied.

3. Short Quotations. A short quotation should not appear as a separate paragraph. It should be enclosed in quotation marks, and included in a paragraph of your manuscript.

4. Long Quotations. A quotation of more than five or six lines should be given as a separate paragraph. Quotation marks are omitted, and the quotation will be printed in smaller type than that used for the text.

Each quotation that is to be printed in small type should be typewritten upon one or more separate sheets of paper that are numbered consecutively with the text pages but bear no text material. The method of preparing the copy is as follows: When the place is reached where a long quotation occurs, remove the text sheet from the typewriter and begin the quotation upon a separate sheet numbered as a new page. Finish typewriting the quotation, using as many sheets as necessary and numbering them as manuscript pages. Then put a new sheet of paper in the typewriter, and continue with the text.

The reason for using this method is that it allows the article to be composed economically on the typesetting machine, which will not set two different sizes of type in one operation. If the manuscript is not prepared in this way, the compositor must handle all of the copy twice, thus needlessly wasting valuable time.

It is advisable to mark clearly the sheets bearing quotations; this may be done by writing the word "Quotation," enclosed in a circle, in the upper left-hand corner.

5. Quotation Within a Quotation. Use single quotation marks for a quotation within a quotation.

Acknowledgments

Acknowledgments of help received from others should be made with simplicity and tact. An effusive acknowledgment may be very embarrassing to your critic or adviser. It is fitting, of course, that mention be made of suggestions, criticisms, or other forms of help that you have received, but this should be done in an appropriate way. The form of acknowledgment and its place in the paper should be determined by the usual practice in the journal in which your article is to be published. Acknowledgment may be made by a brief statement appearing in a footnote to the title of the article. The form for a thesis may be "Prepared in the Department of——, under the direction of Professor——." If persons other than the adviser have helped, mention of the fact may be made in the form of footnotes in the parts of the paper concerned. Another suitable place for acknowledgments is in the introduction to the paper.

Analytical Table of Contents

1. Analylical Outline. Before a manuscript is offered for publication, an analytical outline, or table of contents, should be prepared. Although the outline will not be printed, it has two important uses: (a) It aids you in making the final revisions of your paper, especially in preparing correct headlines. (b) It is almost indispensable to anyone reading your manuscript with the object of criticizing it.

2. Form. The outline that follows will serve as an example of an analytical table of contents. The rank of the headings for the various divisions of an article should be indicated in the table of contents by graded indentations. Note that the principal divisions are begun flush with the left-hand edge of the writing; the subdivisions of the principal divisions are indented five spaces on the typewriter, and smaller subdivisions are indented 10 spaces.

Indicate properly the comparative values of the topics. If two topics are logically coordinate, do not make one topic subordinate to the other. On the other hand, if one topic is logically subordinate to another, do not give them equal value.

Example of analytical table of contents

CONTENTS

Headings in the Text

1. Revising Headings. The analytical outline, prepared as described above, should be used as a basis for revising, if necessary, the headings that appear in the text of your paper, and for indicating the rank of the headings. The editor will mark the manuscript to indicate the sizes and styles of type for headings.

2. Center Headings. In the text, or body of the paper, the headings indicating principal divisions of the article should be typewritten in capitals as center headings. It is best not to underline them on the typewriter; the editor will underscore them with two lines to indicate small caps, or will write "s.c." in the margin. In the example, "Introduction," "Materials and methods," "Experiments and results," "Discussion of results," and "Literature cited" indicate the headings of the main sections of the paper.

But note: (a) The heading "Abstract" is omitted if the abstract is printed in distinctive type; (b) the heading "Introduction" is usually omitted; and (c) the heading "Literature cited" is conveniently printed in capitals of the type used for the citations.

3. Center Subheadings. The headings indicating subdivisions should be typewritten as center headings in small (lower-case) letters; only the first word and proper nouns should have capital initials. Each word should be underlined on the typewriter with a single straight line, to indicate that it is to be printed in italics. In the sample outline, "Plants," "Cultural methods," "Measurement of climatic conditions," etc., indicate the center subheads.

4. Paragraph Side Headings. Still smaller subdivisions should appear as side heads, indented as paragraphs. The side head is "run in"— that is, run together in a continuous line with the paragraph to which it belongs. Only the first word and proper nouns should have capital initials. A single straight line should be typewritten under each word of the side head to indicate that it is to be printed in italics; a period should follow the side head. In the example, "Temperature," "Rainfall," and "Evaporation" indicate the paragraph side heads.

For reasons of economy and appearance, most journals use italic type for side heads, rather than bold-faced type. But to help the reader find topics quickly, this handbook, like many textbooks, uses bold-faced type and capitalizes all important words.

5. Over-minute Subdivision. Excessive subdivision of the text should be avoided, since it confuses rather than aids the reader; three grades (center heads, center subheads, and paragraph side heads) are enough.

In the early drafts of a paper, it is desirable to show clearly the principal divisions and their subdivisions, and so these three grades of headings are usually employed. But in making the final revision for publication, try to avoid the use of center subheads; let the main divisions of the paper appear as center heads, and the subdivisions appear as paragraph side heads. Even center heads should be used sparingly.

6. Styles of Type. The following example shows a style often used for center headings. It has the advantages of being pleasing to the eye, and economical because composed with the text, in one operation.

CENTER HEADINGS (SMALL CAPS OF TEXT TYPE)

Center subheads (lower-case italics of text type)

Another style avoids the use of center headings; only paragraph side headings are used—small caps for main headings and lower-case italics for subheadings. In the preparation of books, it is often necessary to use special styles of headings. For textbooks, bold-faced headings are generally preferred, because they make the topics stand out prominently.

CHAPTER 4

Tables

Usage and Format

1. Importance. The first step in the analysis of experimental data is to arrange them in the form of tables. This part of the work may require a great deal of study before the best scheme for bringing out relations is found. Two general types of tables may be needed: (a) those which contain the original data, including actual observations and measurements, and (b) those which contain derived data, bringing out special points and conclusions. A large part of the work of interpretation of the data will have been completed when well-arranged tables have been made.

2. Unity. Each table should be a unit. A table is a short-cut means of presenting facts to the reader, and a table (like a sentence, paragraph, or article) should present one subject with distinctness. Do not attempt to bring out in a single table several comparisons of very different kinds. Very large tables are likely to be confusing.

3. Clearness. The form of the table should be arranged to secure greatest clearness. For each kind of comparison of data, there is usually one form of table that brings out the comparison most clearly and systematically. In addition to the absolute figures representing original observations, the table may include percentages, ratios, totals, averages, etc.; the latter are often of great value in making comparisons.

4. Accuracy. Every item in the table must be checked for correctness.

5. Economy. Since tables cost much more per page than text material, they should be used only when needed and should not be made unnecessarily large. For a two-column page, they should be designed, if possible, to fit within a single column. Abbreviations should be used to keep the column heads of the table small. A column should not be devoted to only one or two entries, to a repetition of the same entry, or to data that may be easily calculated from data in another column. Such cases can usually be cared for in footnotes or in notes following the title.

6. Size. The table must be compiled so as to fit the page of the publication. On a two-column page, tables may occupy a single column, or, if necessary, the full width of the page. The space that a printed table will require may be estimated by means of character counts. As an approximation, assume that in the 8-point type used for the body of the table there are 17 characters per horizontal inch and 7 lines per vertical inch, and in the 6-point type used for the box heads there are 21 characters per horizontal inch. Allowance must be made for space between columns equal to at least 2 characters.

When large tables are required, the method of handling them should be left to the judgment of the printer. If a table is too large to come within the width of the page, it may be possible to set it lengthwise on the page. If it will fit neither crosswise nor lengthwise, then it may be possible to keep it within bounds by setting it in 6-point type, the smallest size used for book and periodical work. If this method fails, the table may be spread across two facing pages.

A folder should not be used unless it is absolutely unavoidable. Folders are not only very costly, but are unwieldy for the reader and are likely to be torn when handled in the library.

7. Large Tables in Manuscript. If a table requires a larger sheet than that used for the text of the manuscript, the sheet may be folded and inserted in place as one of the manuscript pages.

8. Each Table on Separate Page. Each individual table in a manuscript should be placed on a separate sheet of paper, without any text on the same page. When the place for a table is reached in a manuscript, the remainder of the page or sheet should be left blank, and a new sheet should be used on which the table only appears with its heading and footnotes, if any. The text should be continued on a fresh sheet of paper.

This procedure helps in layout of the text in relation to the table on the final pages prepared for the printer. If later through oversight or otherwise, it becomes necessary to insert a table in a full page of text material, it should be treated as an insert.

9. Open and Ruled Tables. Tables may be either open or ruled; the former generally are used in tables of only two columns, though they are employed exclusively in some periodicals. The suggestions given below refer specifically to ruled tables.

10. Heading, or Title. The tables are numbered consecutively throughout each article. The word "Table," capitalized and followed by an Arabic number, appears as a center heading (printed in 8-point type). The legend, or description, of the table is centered above the body of the table; only the first word and proper names have capital initials; the legend is printed in 8-point italics. In typewriting the legend, each word is underscored with a single straight line to indicate italic type to the printer. The legend should be self-explanatory and should enable the reader to understand the table without referring to the text of the article. It should be broad enough to include all the data in the table. Make it definite—allow only one meaning.

11. Box Heads. The box heads, at the tops of columns in a table, appear in small caps (6-point). The secondary heads, when present, are printed in ordinary type (6-point lower-case), with only the first word having a capital initial.

12. Units of Measurement. Units of quantity are given below the line under the box heads and printed in 6-point italics. (In the stub, or first column, such units are placed on the right, according to a rule sometimes followed.)

13. Body of Table. Columns consisting of words in the body of the table should appear in ordinary type. Figure columns should be aligned on the right; reading columns, on the left. Figure columns should be separated from perpendicular rules at least an en space; decimals should be aligned; figures should be centered in the columns. Omissions should be indicated by blank spaces; the reasons for omissions of important data should be explained in footnotes. If possible, the body of the table is printed in 8-point type on 10-point base; it is sometimes necessary to use 6-point type.

14. Footnotes. Explanatory footnotes to tables are indicated by means of standard footnote reference marks (*, †, ‡, §, etc.) placed after the words or the numbers to which the footnotes refer.[15] The footnotes are typewritten on the sheet bearing the table. Each footnote is preceded by a symbol and is indented as a paragraph. Footnotes are printed in 8-point type on 10-point base.

15. Special Type. Bold-faced and italic type may be used to distinguish different classes of data in a table. Uniform type treatment, however, is desirable. In general, it is well to avoid unnecessary multiplicity of sorts of type.

16. Cross Rules. Care should be taken that as few cross rules as possible are used. A cross rule is necessary at the top of the table, another is needed below the box heads, and a third is needed at the bottom of the table. Any additional cross rules increase the cost of printing. Where a line of demarcation is necessary, it can be indicated effectively and inexpensively by a blank space, which can be composed by the typesetting machine.

17. Spacing. In the printed table, the figure columns should be cast to cover the normal requirements of the figure entries or wording of box heads; spaces between perpendicular rules should, if possible, be the same; the balance of the space may be put in the stub (first column) or other reading columns. Tables should be set leaded. In long tables, grouping the horizontal lines of figures in groups of four lines, by a double lead, makes the table easier to read and aids in preventing inaccurate reading.

18. References in Text. References to tables should be made by number. (For example: By reference to table 10; the data presented in table 3.)

---

15. Lower-case superscript letters are used instead of symbols by many journals. The letters are usually placed *after* the words or *before* the numbers to which the footnotes refer.

CHAPTER 5

Illustrations

Purpose

Illustrations form an integral part of the concise and effective presentation of scientific material. They serve as a short-cut means of presenting descriptive matter and of showing relations among data. By looking at an illustration, the reader gains information that he would otherwise have to procure from a long verbal explanation. He is able to obtain from an illustration a clear conception of objects or relations that are too complex to be adequately described in words. If the paper is suitably illustrated, the text may be largely devoted to comparisons, inferences, and discussion of principles. Photographs and drawings are especially important in the descriptive phases of science. Diagrams of apparatus and graphs of data are mainly required in the experimental and quantitative phases.

The first impression a reader gets of an article is greatly influenced by the appearance of the illustrations. He is likely to receive an unfavorable impression of the whole article if the illustrations are poor. But he is attracted to the article if the illustrations are clear, artistic, and informative. It is very important, therefore, to devote much time and study to the planning and preparation of illustrative material. Each illustration should be a unit, presenting a single subject as clearly and distinctly as possible. Special attention should be given to uniformity in style, tone, and lettering. For putting drawings and graphs into final form, the services of a professional artist or draftsman may be needed.

Correct Proportions

An illustration with dimensions approximating $1 \times 1^1/_2$ is most pleasing to the eye. The appearance of the page is best and the work is facilitated if every illustration has the same width as the type page or type column. For a journal printed in two columns, illustrations should usually be designed to occupy the width of a single column, and should therefore be tall rather than wide.

1. Graphical Method. Figure 1 shows a convenient graphical method of obtaining the correct proportions for an illustration to occupy the full width of a page or column. On a large sheet of Bristol board, or of stiff white cardboard on which a group of drawings or photographs is to be mounted, construct, in pencil, a rectangle, *ABCD,* which is the exact size of the desired reproduction. This rectangle is the same in width as the type page or column but is enough shorter to allow space for the printed legend. Space for the legend may be approximated by counting the number of characters in the legend and then measuring the space occupied by a printed legend with the same number of characters (see page 83). (Some journals allow use of the full height of the page, and print the legend at the foot of the facing page.) Extend the diagonal *AC* as far as you wish on the Bristol board or cardboard. Any point on the diagonal will determine a rectangle that has the correct proportions of width and length. For example, the point *C'* determines the correct rectangle *AB'C'D';* the point *C"* determines the correct rectangle *AB"C"D",* etc.

If the reproduction is to occupy only a part of the width or height of the type page or column, a similar procedure is used. The original, small rectangle is always made the exact size of the intended reproduction.

2. Checking Completed Illustration. A completed illustration may easily be checked to find out whether its height or its width must determine the reduction. Cut a sheet of paper to the size of the type page or type column *minus* the height of the legend. Place it on the illustration in the position of *ABCD* in figure 1, and lay a long ruler on the illustration so as to extend the diagonal *AC.* Then: (a) if the ruler intersects the *side* of the illustration, the *height* must be reduced to that of the type page or column *minus* the height of the legend; or (b) if the ruler intersects the

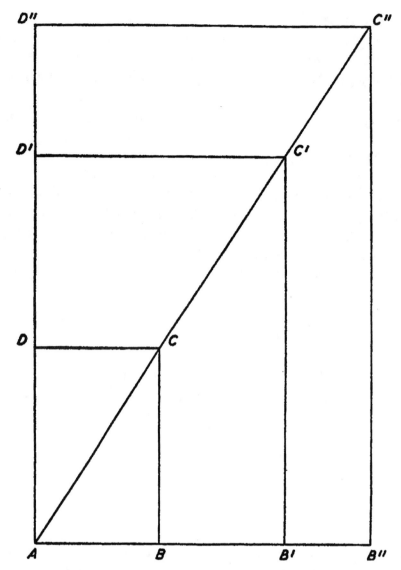

FIG. 1. Method of securing correct proportions for an illustration.

top of the illustration, the *width* must be reduced to that of the type page or column.

Drawings

1. Methods of Reproduction. Drawings are usually produced by the same method as the text. Lines in the drawings should be black, so that they can be readily picked up by the camera used to make the film from which the printing plates are made. In some methods, it is not necessary to produce film, and the camera transmits directly to the printing plate-making equipment. If a pencil is used to prepare the drawing, the drawing should be first reproduced on a copier machine to obtain the black lines, and repair any broken lines with black pen or marker, before submitting to the printer.

2. Plates and Text Figures. Drawings may be used either as plates or as text figures. Plates are often printed on glossy paper as separate pages and may be put at the end of the article. Text figures are printed on the same paper as the text and often have text material above or below them. Many journals use the same paper for all illustrations and prefer to treat them all as text figures. As many figures as desired may be grouped together.

3. Size of Drawing. The width or length of the original drawing should be from two to three times that of the reproduction. Slight inaccuracies in lines become invisible when reduced. Standard enlargements should be used for drawings in the same article, so as to insure ready comparability.

Drawings From Photographs

1. Advantages. A line drawing may be made from a photograph. For illustrating a piece of scientific apparatus, such a drawing may be much better than a photograph, because the drawing shows only the points that are essential and omits unnecessary and confusing details. Hidden parts can be shown by cut-away sections. A very natural perspective may easily be obtained in a drawing based on a photograph. The technique is simpler and quicker than the freehand method. The drawing may be used to illustrate any type of subject matter, and it may be a simple outline or a realistic picture. The final result is limited only by the skill of the draftsman. An excellent drawing may be made from a relatively poor photograph.

2. Method. The simplest way to prepare such a drawing is to trace it from a print made on 8 × 10 inch or larger single-weight paper. A sheet of translucent drawing vellum is placed over the print, and a light is put below it for transillumination. The desired lines are then traced in pencil on the drawing vellum. Details that are not wanted are not traced. It is easy to study the progress of the drawing, and to disassociate it from the photograph, merely by turning off the light and observing the drawing by reflected light alone. Any shading that is desired may be put in with stippling or hatching, as in making ordinary pen drawings. Measurements, explanatory letters, and labels may be inserted.

Graphs

Graphs are designed to portray relations existing among data. They must be accurate, and they should also be clear. Since the ease with which the relations may be seen depends upon unity, balance, and other features of good composition, graphs should be constructed so as to be pleasing to the eye. The suggestions given here are intended as guides to

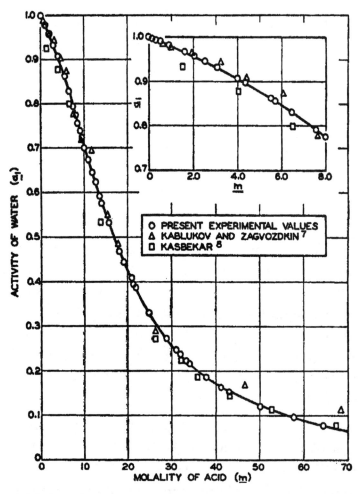

FIG. 2. Activity of water over orthophosphoric acid solutions at 25°C.

84

the achievement of effective presentation. Figures 2–8 exemplify some of these suggestions.

Papers ruled with green, orange, red, yellow, or black lines are unsatisfactory unless it is desired that all lines be reproduced, or unless the graph is to be transferred to white illustrating or Bristol board, white paper, or tracing cloth. If all coordinate lines are to appear in the reproduction, special care should be taken to use a paper in which the lines (preferably black) contrast sharply with the white background.

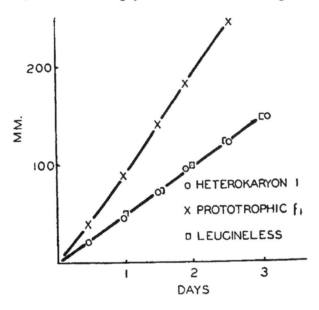

Fig. 3. Growth of a heterokaryon luecineless and adapted *Neurospora crassa* and of the separate components on a limiting concentration of *l*(+)leucine (0.0075 mg./ml.) at 25°C.

1. Size and Proportions. The general suggestions made regarding the size and proportions of illustrations apply to graphs. Proportions of length to width approximating $1:1^1/_2$ are most pleasing in appearance. The length or width of the original graph should be from two to three times that of the desired reproduction.

Many journals prefer to have the reproduction occupy the full width of the type page or the full width of a single column of a two-column page. A part or all the height of the type page may be utilized. The final reproduction should have a large enough scale to show essential details and accommodate necessary numbers and labels.

2. Choice of Coordinates. It is customary to plot the independent variable on the horizontal axis and the dependent variable on the vertical axis. But it is not always possible to distinguish between the two kinds of variables. Intervals of time are plotted on the horizontal axis.

3. Scale of Coordinates. The scale of coordinates should be chosen so that the graph, when reduced to the size required for printing, will be neither crowded nor wasteful of space. It is desirable to use the same scale in a series of comparable graphs. If the graph is to be used as a source of quantitative data, the scale and precision should be such as to allow the coordinates of any point to be read quickly and accurately. But if the graph is presented to illustrate the nature of the relation between two variables, a smaller scale may be used. Many of the graphs in scientific papers are of this type, especially where the original data are presented in tables.

It may be desirable to try to find a method of plotting that will give a straight line; if this can be done, it may give a clue to the mathematical

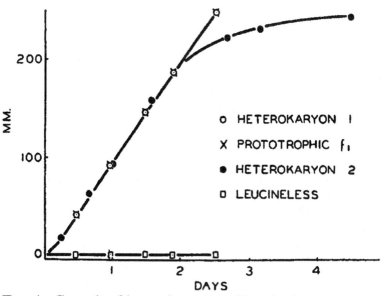

FIG. 4. Growth of heterokaryons of leucineless and adapted *Neurospora crassa* and of the separate components on minimal agar medium devoid of leucine at 25°C.

86

relation between the two variables.[16] If the ordinary graph is straight, the relation follows the linear law ($y = ax + b$); if a log-log graph is straight, it follows the power law ($y = Kx^n$); or if a semilog graph is straight, it follows the compound-interest law ($y = Pe^{rx}$). In many cases, of course, none of these graphs is straight, and the mathematical relation between the two variables is more complex.

It is desirable to choose the coordinates so that the important part of the curve approximates a slope of unity—i.e., makes an angle of about 45° with the horizontal axis.

Round numbers—multiples of 5, 10, 20, etc.—are put on the heavy lines of coordinate paper ruled in the decimal system. In logarithmic plots, either the logarithms of the numbers or the numbers themselves

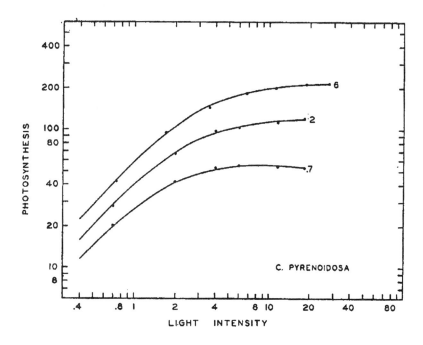

Fig. 5. Rate of photosynthesis (cu.mm. O_2 evolved per hour per 100 million cells) in relation to light intensity (thousands of meter candles) for *Chlorella pyrenoidosa*. Both scales are logarithmic. Cultural intensities are shown by curve labels.

---

16. Many readers, however, prefer curves made from the original data, since they find it difficult to visualize relations when the logarithms of the variables are plotted.

may be used, depending upon which scheme is clearer or more useful. The coordinate scales should be labeled so as to indicate clearly the name of the quantity plotted and the unit of measurement. These labels should be balanced near the middle of the axes and should not be crowded too close to the numbers on the scale. The label on the vertical axis should be oriented so that it is read upward along this axis.

4. Plotting the Points. The points are plotted with a sharp pencil, each point being surrounded by a circle or other symbol. Different symbols, such as open and closed circles, triangles, and squares, may be used to distinguish several curves in the same graph, or several sets of data for a single curve. After the points have been plotted, all should be carefully checked. Observed points should always be clearly shown on the curves. But computed points, plotted from a mathematical equation, should not be shown.

5. Drawing the Curve. Where possible, a smooth curve should be drawn to represent the plotted points. Smoothing shows relations most clearly and minimizes errors. Of course, if the points are widely or irregularly distributed, all that can be done is to connect them with straight lines.

In drawing a smooth curve by hand, use light sweeping strokes with a pencil. Obtain a satisfactory curve by erasure and correction. To detect kinks that require correction, sight with one eye along the curve. The smoothed curve need not pass through all the points, but it should be drawn so that about half the points in a group fall on each side of it.

Some workers like to draw the smoothed curve on a piece of tracing paper held over the graph with drafting tape or rubber cement. The curve may then be transferred to the original by blackening the back of the paper with a soft pencil and tracing over the curve with a hard pencil. Another method of transferring the curve involves mounting the tracing paper with rubber cement on a piece of moderately thick cardboard and then cutting with scissors along the curve. The cardboard template is used in drawing the curve in pencil on the original graph. A very regular curve, free from waviness, may be obtained in this manner.

Several curves may be drawn in the same graph, but they should not be so numerous or so crowded as to make the graph difficult to decipher. The curves may be distinguished by different symbols repre-

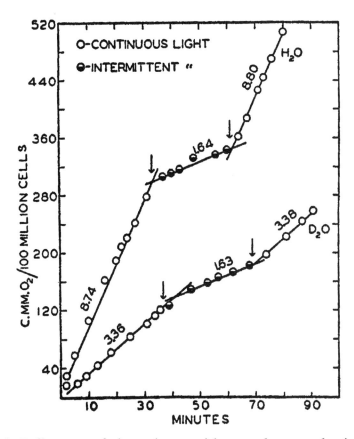

Fig. 6. Influence of deuterium oxide on photosynthesis of *Chlorella vulgaris* in continuous and in intermittent illumination. Numbers above curves are rates per minute.

senting the points and by different kinds of lines—solid, long dash, short dash, dot and dash, etc. The individual curves may be designated by capital letters (usually italic) or preferably by distinctive labels along the curves. The curves can be identified by means of a key placed in a balanced position in the graph, or by reference in the figure legend to the explanatory letters or to the types of lines and symbols.

If it has been necessary to plot the graph on coordinate paper ruled with orange or green lines that are not wanted in the reproduction, the graph must be transferred to white illustrating board or three-ply Bristol board (by means of needle pricks), or to translucent bond paper or tracing cloth, before it is inked. A convenient table for use in tracing graphs may be easily constructed by cutting a rectangular opening (17 by 22 inches) in a table and mounting above the opening a countersunk sheet of ground plate-glass (20 by 25 inches); the glass may be illuminated by a 300-watt lamp in a goose-neck stand resting on the floor, or by suitably placed fluorescent lamps.

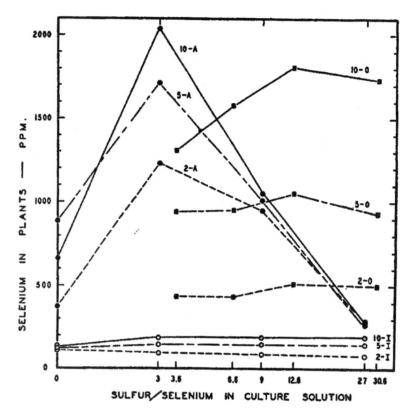

FIG. 7. Selenium accumulation by maize in relation to sulfur/selenium ration (in ppm.) in the culture solution. (Log scale of abscissas except the zero.)

Cultures received 2, 5, and 10 ppm. of selenium as selenate (*A*), selenite (*I*), or organic selenium (*O*) from an *Astragalus* extract. Sulfur supplied as sulfate.

6. Inking the Graph. Inking in the graph is the part of the work that is best done by a professional draftsman. India ink must always be used. The symbol surrounding each point is inked first; it should be about three times as wide as the curve that will be drawn; the point at the center of the symbol is not inked. Circles are made with a compass, preferably of the type known as a drop bow pen; squares and triangles are made with a lettering pen and guide. Lines are drawn with a ruling pen. Straight lines are drawn with the aid of a transparent triangle or

90

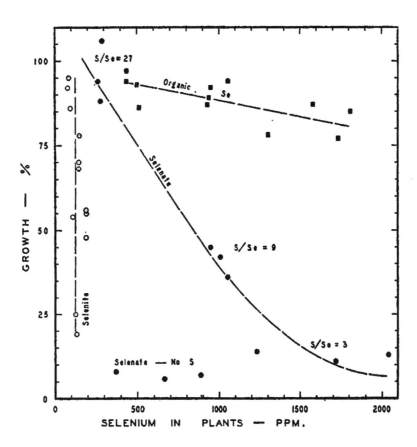

Fig. 8. Relation of growth to selenium content of maize supplied with selenium as selenate, selenite, and organic selenium (derived from extract of *Astragalus*).

straight-edge. Difficulty caused by the ink's running under the triangle may be avoided by putting some strips of adhesive tape on the lower side of the triangle.

Smoothed curves may be drawn most easily with the aid of a flexible curve ruler, which may be bent to the shape of almost any curve and will retain its form until further distorted. It has the added advantage of being so constructed that the ink will not run under its edge. Curves may also be drawn with the aid of French curves, elevated from the paper by strips of adhesive tape. For best appearance, the curve should not run through the point symbols but should be drawn to join them, or it may even be separated from them by short breaks.

Points falling on the axes should rest in small gaps left in these

91

lines. Where a series of points fall along the horizontal axis, it is best to depress the line representing that axis to some negative value.

The lines representing the axes of the graph should be about the same in width as the heaviest curve, and wider than the coordinates. The lines should be uniform in all the graphs appearing in one article. Full coordinate lines may be drawn, or the coordinates may be indicated by short stubs running in from the axes. The appearance is usually best if the entire graph is framed in a rectangle; but in some cases it may be preferable to leave the graph open at the top and at the right.

Letters and numbers should be made with lines that are somewhat thinner than those used for the axes and curves.

Some publishers take care of all numbering and lettering on graphs. In this case, the author is expected to provide each graph with a tracing-paper overlay, fastened with rubber cement or paste to the upper margin of the back of the copy and folded down over the face. Numbers and letters should be written in pencil on the overlay in the exact places where they are to appear on the graph. The style of letters, whether Roman or italic (vertical or slant), should be indicated by instructions written on the margins of the graph or tracing-paper overlay.

Other publishers expect the author to care for numbering and lettering within the graph, but they have the numbers and labels on the coordinate axes set up in type by the printer. The author should place them in pencil outside the axes.

Corrections in the inked graphs may be made by careful erasing and redrawing, or by pasting a strip of paper over the original and then redrawing. Small irregularities may be removed with an etching knife or by application of pure white pigment (white-out). Retouching may be done with a fine pen. After the graph is finished, it should be gently cleaned with a soft eraser, being careful not to lighten the ink lines.

Photographs

1. Books. Making good photographs for scientific illustration requires familiarity with the rudiments of photographic technique. Skill is easily gained through practice.

2. Background and Composition. The principal subject of the photograph should be shown as clearly and sharply as possible, and non-essential objects should be subordinated or excluded. The background should be unobtrusive; it should be free from distracting lines or spots and preferably of a uniform tone—white, gray, or black—that contrasts sufficiently with the subject. Light backgrounds are usually more attractive than dark ones. Even a light-toned object may show its form and detail best on a white or gray background. The objects in the picture should be arranged so as to give a simple and effective composition. Tones of light and shade should be balanced. Point of view and perspective are important. A worm's-eye or a bird's-eye view may sometimes be both effective and pleasing.

3. Illumination. Modeling and texture should be brought out by differential lighting. In photographing scientific specimens, left-hand illumination is recommended, because we are accustomed to visualize objects as lighted in that way. If photographs of a series of specimens are to be mounted together, illumination in all should come from the same direction; otherwise, elevations may be mistaken for depressions, or vice versa.

The following conventional arrangement of lights is excellent for many scientific subjects: The stronger light (twice the weaker) is placed about 45 degrees to the left of the camera and 45 degrees above it, and the weaker light is placed at the same distance from the object, but level with the camera and considerably less than 45 degrees to the right of it. The same arrangement of lights may be used when the camera is in either the horizontal or vertical position.

Although this simple system of illumination is usually satisfactory, it should be modified as much as necessary to suit the particular subject. The important point is to arrange the illumination so that the negative will faithfully record the outline, form, tone values, and details (in both shadows and highlights) of the original subject.

4. Copy for Reproduction. Photographs are reproduced as halftones, in which the picture is broken up into minute dots. The photograph for copy should be as clear and sharp as possible. It may be considerably larger than the reproduction, or the same size, but should never be smaller.

If a print needs to be retouched, it should be of large size—5 × 7 or 8 × 10 inches.

Loss of fine detail is inevitable in reproduction by the half-tone process. To compensate for this loss, the scale of magnification must be larger in a half-tone than would be satisfactory in a glossy photographic print. For example, if one-fourth natural size is a sufficiently great magnification to show an object well in a glossy print, double this magnification—or one-half natural size—may be required in a half-tone to make the object equally clear. Use close-ups of essential features; and in making the print, enlarge sufficiently and then crop away all extraneous parts of the photograph.

Glossy white ferrotyped paper is best for prints intended for reproduction. A paper with a pebbled or rough surface, or a cream color, should never be used.

If much retouching is necessary, some workers prefer a print with a smooth or semi-matte surface But a glossy print may be prepared so that it will accept retouching. The purpose of such preparation is chiefly to remove any invisible greasy finger marks that have come from handling. The simplest method is to sift Fuller's earth or talc on the print and then to rub this lightly over the whole surface of the print with a dry cotton tuft or soft cloth. Rubbing must be very light, or the print may show scratches. This method is suitable for prints that already bear retouching and for those that are either mounted or unmounted. Those who do much work of this kind prefer to prepare glossy prints by rubbing over the whole surface with a moist cotton swab that has been previously rubbed on a cake of gelatin. The cake is prepared by dissolving ordinary gelatin (obtainable at a drugstore) in boiling water, adding one drop of glacial acetic acid to about 30 grams of gelatin, and allowing the solution to evaporate in a small container so that it forms a cake. This treatment can be used only on a mounted print that has had no previous retouching; moisture of course would make an unmounted print curl and would smudge one that had been retouched.

5. Contrast of Print. The print for reproduction should preserve as closely as possible the details that exist in the original subject. It is desirable to have the print show a wide range of tone values, with detail in both shadows and highlights. A good procedure is to make a series of prints on several contrast grades of paper, and then to select the print that seems best. The usual method of selecting the proper contrast grade of paper for a normal print is to make a test print that gives the desired highlight gradations. Then: (a) if the shadows are also correct, the paper is of the right contrast grade; (b) if the shadows are blocked by over-exposure, use a less contrasty paper; (c) if the shadows are not dark enough, use a more contrasty paper.

Special requirements of the half-tone process indicate the desirability of a slight modification of the usual procedure in print making. A print for reproduction should not make use of the full range of tone values from clear white to jet black. The reason for this recommendation is that the rendering of detail at both ends of the tone scale is unavoidably degraded; the density-exposure gradient is less at the extremes of the characteristic curve of papers than in the middle-tone region of the curve. A print of slightly softened quality is therefore recommended.

6. Blemishes. Blemishes in a print will be conspicuous in the reproduction. Imperfections of this sort include blurred images, muddy highlights, fog, spots, scratches, dents, cracks, and stains. A defective print should be replaced by one that is perfect. If this is impossible, skillful retouching by an artist may remove minor defects; but this work is expensive and the results are likely to be unsatisfactory.

If it is necessary to write on the back of a photograph, lay the print on a smooth, hard surface (such as a sheet of glass) and write very lightly with a soft pencil; unless care is taken, the writing will show in relief on the face of the print. A better method is to write on a separate strip of paper and attach this with dry mounting tissue to the margin on the back of the print.

7. Arrangement in Groups. When a number of separate photographs are to be arranged together for half-tone reproduction in a single plate, they should be carefully matched for uniformity of density and contrast. If the group consists of some light and some dark prints or includes prints that differ in contrast, these differences may be accentuated in the reproduction.

The selected prints should be trimmed and mounted with special care.[17] The cut edges of the prints always show in the half-tone reproduc-

17. If the publisher prefers to do the mounting in groups, the prints should be supplied untrimmed and unmounted.

tion; and unless the edges are straight, the background will have to be routed out, thus doubling or trebling the cost of reproduction.

8. Models. It will be useful to study as models the photographs that are published in the scientific journals. Critical examination will show good and poor pictures that serve to emphasize the points briefly discussed here. Perhaps the best examples of highly effective photography are those that appear in current advertising material and inexpensive booklets issued by manufacturers of apparatus, instruments, and photographic materials.

Preparing Illustration Copy

1. Identification. For purposes of identification, the figure number, the author's name and address, and the title of the article should be written on the margin or back of each piece of illustration copy, or on a piece of paper attached securely with paste to the lower margin of the copy. The "top" of the illustration should be indicated if there is any possibility of misunderstanding.

2. Directions for Reduction. Clear directions for reduction should also be written on the margin or back. In giving directions, it is best to specify the final width or height. (For example: "Reduce width to $4^{1}/_{2}$ inches" or "reduce height to 6 inches.") In designating fractional reduction, it is better to say "reduce width to $^{1}/_{4}$" than "reduce $^{3}/_{4}$ or $^{3}/_{4}$ off."

3. Photographic Copies. If the illustrations are larger than $8^{1}/_{2}$ by 11 inches, duplicate photographic prints or photostats of smaller size should accompany the manuscript, to facilitate sending the article to reviewers.

Retain a good photographic copy of each illustration, for use if the original is lost in the mail.

The original is best for making a photoengraving. A very good photographic copy may be used. But a copy that is out of square (not rectangular) or faint is not acceptable.

4. Legends. The legends, or titles, of plates and figures should be self-explanatory. They should be typewritten *double-spaced* in numerical order upon one or more sheets of paper, placed at the end of the manuscript following the literature cited. Always supply a short title for the illustration. Any descriptive matter should follow directly after this title, in the form of paragraphs.

The legend of each text figure is printed below the figure. A short title appears below each plate, and complete descriptions of all plates are usually given in a separate section of the paper, following the literature cited and preceding the plates.

Shipping Illustrations

Photographic prints or drawings intended for half-tone reproduction are likely to be damaged when sent by mail or express unless they are well protected, especially at the corners. The following method of wrapping gives good protection: Place the prints between sheets of thin cardboard, cut to a size slightly larger than the prints. (If the prints are mounted, cover them with a sheet of thin cardboard of the same size as that on which they are mounted.) Bind the cardboard sheets together on all four sides with short strips of cellulose tape. Anchor this packet securely, with more strips of cellulose tape, to a piece of stout corrugated board about two inches larger all around than the original packet. This will keep the packet from slipping to an edge or corner. Place another piece of corrugated board of the same size on top (preferably one with the corrugations running at right angles to those of the other), and bind the two firmly together with strips of cellulose tape. Finally, wrap in heavy paper, and seal all loose edges with gummed tape or tie securely with string.

CHAPTER 6

Prepublication Review / Steps

Process

1. Purposes. Many scientific journals have adopted the plan of having every paper that is submitted for publication read and criticized by two competent reviewers selected by the editor or the editorial committee. The purposes of this procedure are (1) to improve the quality of the papers that are printed in the journal and (2) to avoid the acceptance of material more rapidly than it can be published with the funds available by promoting condensation of text and tabular material and elimination of unessential illustrations, as well as by declining the papers that make the least distinct contributions to the particular field of science. Since all papers are sent to reviewers, this procedure implies no reflection on the merits of the papers. Prepublication review represents an editorial service that the authors appreciate in the majority of cases.

2. Work of Reviewers. Each reviewer is asked to give his general opinion regarding the suitability of the paper for publication in the journal, and to make specific suggestions regarding possible errors, lack of clearness, parts that may be condensed, omitted, or improved in form and arrangement, etc. The reviewer may be asked the following questions:

(a) Would you grade the paper A, B, C, D, or E, on the basis of its relative merit as a scientific contribution—if C represents the average rank of papers in recent volumes of the journal? (b) Has the material been published previously? (c) Has the work been carried far enough to warrant publication? (d) Is there some other journal for which the paper would be more suitable? (e) Are the conclusions logical and are they based on accurate and sufficient data? (f) Is the arrangement logical? If not, suggest improvements. (g) Which, if any, of the main ideas are not developed with sufficient emphasis? (h) What parts may be condensed or omitted? (i) Have you found any errors in the paper? (j) Is there lack of clearness? If so, where? (k) Where does the literary form need to be improved? (l) What improvements, if any, do you regard as necessary in the illustrations? (m) Which, if any, of the illustrations could be omitted?

3. Author's Revision. If the reviews indicate that the article would be acceptable but needs revision, it is returned to the author with the comments of the reviewers (quoted anonymously so that the matter of personalities will not enter) and a note that asks the author to study the paper again with regard to revision in accordance with the reviewers' suggestions. The author is told that if he does not consider it desirable to adopt certain of the recommendations of the reviewers, the reasons for his preference should be explained. When the paper has been revised by the author, it is returned to the editor.

4. Judgment of a Third Reviewer. Advice of a third reviewer may be asked by the editors if the two reviewers disagree as to whether the paper would be acceptable after revision, or if the author is unwilling to revise the paper in accordance with the reviewers' recommendations. The opinions of reviewers are advisory, and final responsibility for the selection of papers rests with the editor.

5. Publication after Acceptance. After its acceptance the paper is published in its proper turn, according to the original date of receipt, unless revisions necessitate unavoidable delay.

6. Rejection of Manuscripts. The editor may decide, after seeing the reviewers' comments and reading the paper himself, that the paper could not be accepted even if it were revised. In this case he returns it to the author with a brief note of regret, containing suggestions, if possible, regarding suitable journals to which the article might be submitted. The editor obviously must not accept material more rapidly than it can be published with the funds available. With the aid of the reviewers and the editorial committee, he selects the papers that seem to be best, and he is compelled to reject the others.

CHAPTER 7

Proofreading

Method

1. Two Persons. If possible, have another person slowly read aloud from the manuscript, while you follow the page proofs and make the necessary corrections and changes. The one who reads aloud should call your attention to every paragraph, mark of punctuation, capitalized word, italicized figure or word, bold-faced figure or word, etc., and should spell out all unusual names or technical terms. If you cannot secure the services of another person in this work, then it will be necessary for you to compare carefully the page proofs with the manuscript, line by line or sentence by sentence.

2. Two Readings. Always read the proofs *twice,* at least.

Proofreading Symbols

Mark Made in Margin	Explanation	How Indicated in the Copy

1. Marks of Instruction

℘	delete, take out	She sold the book.
sold ∧	insert	She the book.
ⓢⓟ	spell out	She sold 10 copies.
ⓉⓇ	transpose	She the sold book.
¶	paragraph	...read. She sold the book.
Ⓡⓤⓝ-ⓘⓝ	run together	read. She sold the book.
new line	new line	She sold books in: Paris, NY...
stet	leave as it stands	She sold the book.
⌒//	use a slash to separate proofreading symbols and to indicate number of repetitions	She sold the book pens and pencils.

2. Marks Regarding Type Style

ital.	set in *italics*	She sold the book.
ⓑⓕ	set in **boldface**	She sold the book.
ⓤⓛ	underline	She sold the book.
Rom	change from *italic* to roman	She sold the book.
cap	set in Capital	she sold the book.
l.c.	set in lowercase	She sold the book.
U|L	set in upper and lowercase	SHE SOLD THE BOOK.
ⓢⓒ	set in SMALL CAPS	She sold the book.
⌄3	superscript	xy3/
⌃2	subscript	H_2O

3. Marks Regarding Defects in Type

broken type	broken letters	She sold the book.
w.f.	wrong font	She sold the book.
‖	align vertically	She sold the book. He sold the book, too.
═══	align horizontally	She sold the book.

4. Marks Regarding Spacing

⌒ ⌣	close up	She s old the book.

Mark Made in Margin	Explanation	How Indicated in the Copy
℘	delete and close up	She sold the boozk.
#	insert space	She sold thebook.
→⌐	indent	She sold the book.
⌐ ⌐	center	⌐STUPID PET TRICKS⌐ 1. The Froggy Broad Jump 2. Cat Ventriloquism
⊑	move left as indicated	She sold the book.
	move right as indicated	She sold the book.
⌐ ⌐	raise as indicated	She sold the book.
⌐ ⌐	lower as indicated	She sold the book.
eq #	correct spacing between letters	She sold the book.
leading	correct spacing between lines	She sold the book. He read the book she sold.

5. Marks of Punctuation

*See section 4.2.1-4.2.3 for proper use of dashes and hyphens

⊙	period	She sold the book.
˄	comma	She sold the book and went on her way.
˄	semicolon	She sold the book she always manages to sell books.
⊙	colon	For example ten books, four tapes...
˅	apostrophe	It is the authors copy.
˅ / ˅˅	open and close quotes	She said: Forget what you have to do.
|/ ?/	exclamation point question mark	Stop the presses Did they stop the presses
⊜	equal sign	SILENCE DEATH
=	hyphen*	He generated a printout.
⊥/N	one-en dash*	Pages 2, 5, and 26 89 are ruined.
⊥/M	one-em dash*	She went with the book.
⊄ / ⊅	open and close parentheses	She Lisa sold the book.
⊄ / ⊅	open and close brackets	She selled sic the book.

102